Scenic Driving

NEW HAMPSHIRE

Exploring the State's Most Spectacular
Byways and Back Roads

STEWART M. GREEN

Globe
Pequot

Guilford, Connecticut

Globe
Pequot

An imprint of Rowman & Littlefield

Distributed by NATIONAL BOOK NETWORK

Copyright © 2016 by Rowman and Littlefield

Photography by Stewart M. Green

Excerpted from *Scenic Routes & Byways New England* (Globe Pequot, 978-0-7627-7955-0)

British Library Cataloguing in Publication Information Available

Library of Congress Cataloging-in-Publication Data Available

ISBN 978-1-4930-2243-4 (paperback)
ISBN 978-1-4930-2244-1 (e-book)

♾™ The paper used in this publication meets the minimum requirements of American National Standard for Information Sciences—Permanence of Paper for Printed Library Materials, ANSI/NISO Z39.48-1992.

TABLE OF CONTENTS

New Hampshire

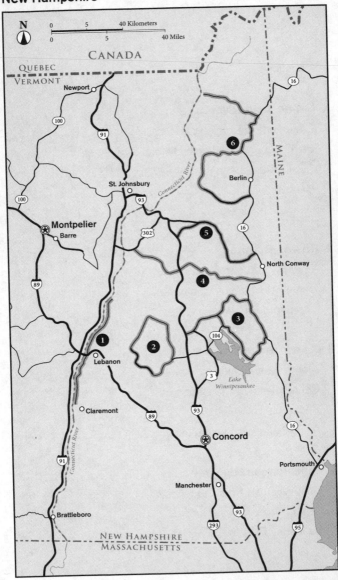

INTRODUCTION

New Hampshire offers travelers a spectacular assortment of natural and scenic wonders, historic sites, and varied recreational opportunities. Numerous state parks, forests, and recreation areas preserve slices of superlative landscapes. In addition to the parks, thousands of lakes and ponds and numerous rivers and brooks offer boating, swimming, canoeing, and angling choices for outdoor enthusiasts. The cities, towns, and villages, from the urban center of Manchester, to myriad tiny villages dotting the hills of New Hampshire, are filled with culture and steeped in history.

Scenic Driving New Hampshire, an indispensable mile-by-mile highway companion, explores and discovers the wonders of this compact region. The drives follow miles of highways and back roads, sampling the region's colorful history, beauty spots, hidden wonders, and scenic jewels. Drivers will wind through the valleys and hills of New Hampshire, marvel at classic villages set between mountains, pass rural birthplaces and burial sites of the notable and the notorious, and wander amid enchanting forests. Most of the drives leave the urban sprawl and interstate highways behind, setting off into the beautiful heart of the region.

New Hampshire is laced with highways and roads, some dating back to the earliest paths that once connected colonial settlements. Area natives will undoubtedly wonder why some roads are included and others omitted. These routes were chosen for their beauty, unique natural history, and historical implications. Omitted are worthy roads for one reason or another, but mostly due to the burgeoning development along those asphalt corridors in an amazing labyrinth of highway possibilities.

Use these described drives to win a new appreciation and understanding of this marvelous land. Take them as a starting point to embark on new adventures by seeking out other back-road gems among the rolling hills and historic towns of New Hampshire.

Travel Advice

Be prepared for changing weather when traveling these scenic highways, especially in winter when snow and ice encase the roadways. Most of the drives, except for bits and pieces, are paved two-lane highways that are regularly maintained. Services are available on almost all the drives, and every little village offers at least some basics during daylight hours. Use caution when driving. Many of the roads twist and wind through valleys and over mountains, with blind corners. Follow the posted speed limits and stay in your lane. Use occasional pullouts to allow faster traffic to safely pass. Watch for heavy traffic on some roads, particularly during summer vacation season and on fall-foliage weekends. Be extremely alert for animals crossing the asphalt. Take care at dusk, just after darkness falls, and in the early morning.

The region's fickle weather creates changeable and dangerous driving conditions. Make sure your windshield wipers are in good shape. Heavy rain can impair highway vision and cause your vehicle to hydroplane. Snow and ice slicken mountain highways. Slow down, carry chains and a shovel, and have spare clothes and a sleeping bag when traveling in winter. Watch for fog and poor visibility, particularly along the coastlines. Know your vehicle and its limits when traveling and, above all, use common sense.

Travelers are, unfortunately, potential crime victims. Use caution when driving in urban areas or popular tourist destinations. Keep all valuables, including wallets, purses, cameras, and video cameras, out of sight in a parked car. Better yet, take them with you when leaving the vehicle.

These drives cross a complex mosaic of private and public land. Respect private property rights by not trespassing or crossing fences.

Remember also that all archaeological and historic sites are protected by federal law. Campers should try to use established campgrounds or campsites whenever possible to avoid adverse environmental impacts. Remember to douse your campfires and to pack all your trash out with you to the nearest refuse container.

Every road we travel offers its own promise and special rewards. Remember Walt Whitman's poetic proclamation as you drive along these scenic highways: "Afoot, light-hearted, I take to the open road. Healthy, free, the world before me."

Legend

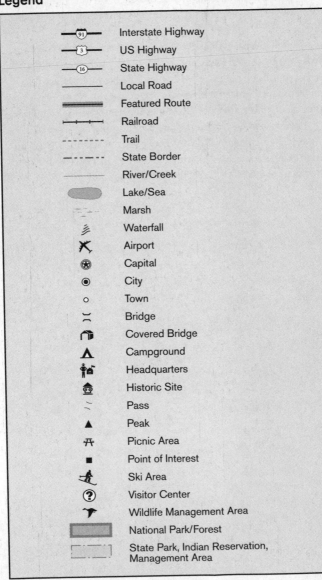	Interstate Highway
	US Highway
	State Highway
	Local Road
	Featured Route
	Railroad
	Trail
	State Border
	River/Creek
	Lake/Sea
	Marsh
	Waterfall
	Airport
	Capital
	City
	Town
	Bridge
	Covered Bridge
	Campground
	Headquarters
	Historic Site
	Pass
	Peak
	Picnic Area
	Point of Interest
	Ski Area
	Visitor Center
	Wildlife Management Area
	National Park/Forest
	State Park, Indian Reservation, Management Area

1 Connecticut River

General description: A 41-mile scenic route along the pastoral Connecticut River Valley between Claremont and Orford in western New Hampshire.

Special attractions: Cornish-Windsor Covered Bridge, Saint-Gaudens National Historic Site, Connecticut River, Dartmouth College, Hood Museum of Art, Orford Street Historic District, Appalachian Trail, scenic views, fishing, hiking, nature study.

Location: Western New Hampshire.

Drive route numbers: NH 12A and 10.

Travel season: Year-round.

Camping: No campgrounds along the drive. Nearby campgrounds in Vermont include Mount Ascutney State Park (39 campsites and 10 lean-to sites) northwest of Ascutney (VT) and Quechee Gorge State Park (45 campsites and 7 lean-to sites) just west of White River Junction and Lebanon.

Services: All services in Claremont, Lebanon, and Hanover. Limited services in towns along the drive including Plainfield, Lyme, and Orford.

Nearby attractions: Cardigan State Park, Sculptured Rocks Natural Area, Mount Sunapee State Park, Gile State Forest, White Mountain National Forest, Bedell Bridge State Park, Mount Ascutney State Park (VT), Quechee Gorge State Park (VT), Woodstock (VT).

The Route

The 41-mile Connecticut River Scenic Route explores some of New Hampshire's most charming scenery as it winds through hill country along the east bank of the mighty Connecticut River in the Upper Valley. The rural secondary roads along the drive pass not only superb views, but also some of New Hampshire's famed cultural and historic shrines including the home of Augustus Saint-Gaudens, perhaps the 19th century's greatest American sculptor;

Connecticut River

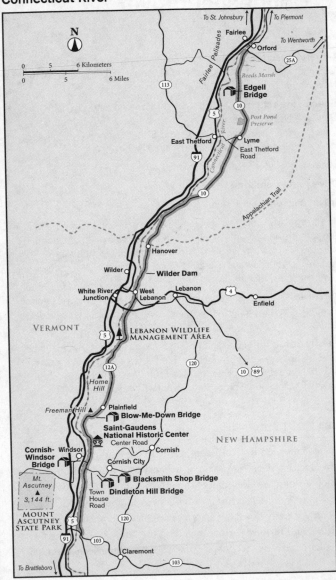

the longest covered bridge in the United States at Cornish; and the beautiful Orford Street Historic District at the drive's northern end.

The **Connecticut River,** New England's longest and largest river, cleaves the region politically, forming the boundary between New Hampshire and Vermont, and geologically. Some geologists interpret the zone that the river follows as a tectonic boundary between two crustal plates—North American bedrock on the west and a slice of an exotic plate from Europe or Africa on the east. The river existed well before the long glacial episodes that have intermittently covered and shaped New England's topography. The last episode, called the Wisconsin glaciation, choked the valley with ice and chiseled it deeper into underlying bedrock.

The Connecticut River, forming the boundary between New Hampshire and Vermont, is New England's largest and longest river.

Later, as the glaciers melted, the valley was filled by Lake Hitchcock, a long, thin lake that stretched 200 miles north from the moraine that blocked the river's course near Middletown, Connecticut. Sediment and silt deposited in the lake by the melting glacier allow geologists to study the rate of glacial recession from New England. Studies of the distinctly laminated varved clays, each layer representing a single year's deposit, show that it took 4,300 years at an average of 245 feet annually for the glacier to recede from Middletown to St. Johnsbury, Vermont. Much of the drive crosses terraced floodplains above the riverbanks.

Claremont to Cornish

The drive begins just west of **Claremont** at the junction of NH 12A and 103. This junction is on the east side of the Connecticut River opposite exit 8 on I-91 and Ascutney, Vermont. The journey's first leg, following NH 12A, travels 18 miles north from here to the southern outskirts of West Lebanon.

The rural highway runs north along the river's east bank past orderly cornfields, apple orchards, and rich farmlands studded with strikingly plain barns and adjoining houses. Low, undulating hills border the riparian floodplain to the east. Pyramid-shaped **Mount Ascutney,** a 3,144-foot peak, looms above the valley to the west in Vermont. This dominating mountain, standing alone and aloof, is a monadnock or high point that towers almost 2,000 feet above the lower, older erosional surface that surrounds it. Ascutney's summit is reached by a 3.8-mile, paved toll road in Mount Ascutney State Park. The mountain is formed of igneous rocks that are part of the White Mountain magma series deposited some 200 million years ago. The mountain's commanding height along the Atlantic Flyway makes the peak a popular spot for birds and

American flags mark the aging gravestones of Revolutionary War soldiers and patriots in the old cemetery next to the Lyme Congregational Church.

The 449-foot Cornish-Windsor Bridge over the Connecticut River is the nation's longest covered bridge.

birders. The state park offers 39 campsites and 10 lean-to sites and an excellent trail to Mount Ascutney's apex.

At 4.2 miles the drive route passes the private **Chase House,** the 1808 birthplace of Salmon Portland Chase. Educated at nearby Dartmouth, Chase defended runaway slaves as a lawyer before becoming an Ohio senator and governor, helping found the Republican Party, and serving as Lincoln's secretary of the treasury and chief justice of the United States. Other old homes dating from the 1770s also line the road.

About 0.5 mile later the road enters **Cornish.** Two covered bridges lie just east of this village on Town House Road. The first, Dingleton Hill Bridge, is 78 feet long. The second, Blacksmith Shop Bridge, spans 96 feet across Mill Brook and was built in 1881. Back on the highway, the drive reaches New Hampshire's most famous covered bridge in another mile. The **Cornish-Windsor Bridge** (or the Windsor-Cornish Bridge, depending on what side of the river you're on) is the longest covered bridge in the country. The 449-foot, two-span bridge, one of the most photographed bridges in America, was built in 1866 at the cost of $9,000. It was engineered and constructed by James Tasker, a construction genius who couldn't read or write. Tasker used heavy, squared timbers rather than thinner planks to form the lattice-work, making a very strong design. Today's bridge, a designated National Historic Civil Engineering Landmark, is the fourth one on the site.

The bridge was the next-to-last Connecticut River bridge to charge a toll. The cost was 2 cents on foot, 4 cents for a horse, 2 cents for a cow, 15 cents to tote a cord of wood across, and 20 cents for a four-horse carriage. A sign across the bridge entrance still says: WALK YOUR HORSE OR PAY TWO DOLLARS FINE. Over time the state of New Hampshire slowly bought out the bridge companies and opened them for free passage, a popular move to discontinue what was called "interstate holdup." The last toll on the Cornish Bridge was collected on May 31, 1943. The next day the bridge was ceremoniously opened for nonpaying customers.

The bridge is still open for traffic and is now a popular tourist stop. Pull off at the designated parking area just south of the bridge and walk up to have a look inside. Vendors across the highway sell postcards, drawings, and other bridge paraphernalia.

Windsor, the historic town on the other side of the river, is acclaimed as the Birthplace of Vermont. New Hampshire, as part of its boundary agreement with Vermont, owns the Connecticut River to its west-bank, normal high-water mark.

Saint-Gaudens National Historic Site

Two miles north of the bridge is another unique and important historic site. Turn right at a park sign and follow a short uphill road for 0.6 mile to **Saint-Gaudens National Historic Site.** The site, operated by the National Park Service from May through October, preserves the elegant hilltop home and studio of Augustus Saint-Gaudens, the premier American sculptor of the 19th century. Born in Ireland and reared in New York City,

Saint-Gaudens worked as an apprentice cameo cutter as a teenager before studying in Paris. He returned to New York and in 1876 at age 27 he received his first commission, the Farragut Monument in today's Madison Square Park. In 1885 he found this lovely spot above the Connecticut River and bought it as a summer residence. Here he executed some of his most famous works, including the *Standing Lincoln,* a Robert Louis Stevenson memorial relief, and the *Shaw Memorial,* a brilliant Civil War relief of Colonel Robert Gould Shaw and his Fifty-fourth Massachusetts Black Volunteer Regiment that took 14 years of exacting work.

The site is scattered with various replicas of Saint-Gaudens's heroic works, sketches, drawings, and casting molds. Visitors can tour the sculptor's house, studio, and exhibition room along with 150 acres of manicured formal gardens and the small Greek temple where Saint-Gaudens is buried. From his deathbed on August 13, 1907, he looked out a window at sunset toward Mount Ascutney and said, "It's very beautiful, but I want to go farther away."

Cornish to Lebanon

Back on the drive, NH 12A passes a historic marker for the **Cornish Colony.** In the latter part of the 19th century, Saint-Gaudens's presence made the rural Cornish area into a thriving artists' colony. Some of the creative artists who lived at the Cornish Colony were the nation's most popular novelist, Winston Churchill (not the British prime minister), and painter Maxfield Parrish. One of Churchill's novels, *Richard Carvell,* sold more than a million copies. The writer hosted President Theodore Roosevelt's 1902 visit to Cornish. Parrish used the surrounding landscape in his colorful, fanciful illustrations for numerous books and magazine covers. Other luminaries who lived and worked

The hilltop home and studio of acclaimed 19th-century sculptor Augustus Saint-Gaudens is preserved as a National Historic Site.

here were sculptor Herbert Adams, poet Percy McKaye, architect Charles A. Platt, and artist Kenyon Cox.

The highway continues north past small Freeman's Cemetery and a side road that leads to **Tasker's Blow-Me-Down Bridge,** a 90-foot covered bridge over Blow-Me-Down Brook. The bridge name is a Yankee corruption of the name Blomidon, an early settler. Past the turn, the roadway bends away from the river to the 1761 village of **Plainfield.** A red-brick community church topped by a white spire dominates the residential town.

A series of low wooded hills—Freeman Hill, Stevens Hill, Home Hill, and Short Knoll—separate the highway from the river as it journeys northward. The road crests a low rise between two hills and drops through forest alongside Beaver Brook to the river. Here it flattens and runs through thick pine and hardwood forests interrupted by occasional floodplain farms. Hills hem the road in on the east, keeping it along the riverbank. At Bloods Brook the highway passes **Lebanon Wildlife Management Area,** a swamp studded with cattails and twisted dead tree trunks. The road passes a gravel quarry and enters the southern outskirts of West Lebanon.

The next 6 miles are mostly developed. The drive continues along NH 12A under I-89 and enters West Lebanon. In the town center, go straight on NH 10 toward Hanover. For a short distance the drive emerges back into bucolic farm country. A roadside picnic area overlooks Wilder Dam and its accompanying hydroelectric plant. Nearby is the Pine Grove Rim Trail. After 3 more miles the highway enters Hanover.

Hanover

Hanover, home of **Dartmouth College,** remains a bastion of culture and diversity in what seems like the New Hampshire

The Lebanon Wildlife Management Area is a riverside swamp filled with tall grass, cattails, and birdsong.

backwoods. The college motto, *Vox Clamantis in Deserto* or "A Voice Cries in the Wilderness," reflects this still-remote character. The college offers a classic Ivy League campus with a grassy quad surrounded by impressive buildings and spreading maple trees. The town of Hanover, originally a farming village, was granted in 1761. The college came 8 years later when Eleazar Wheelock decided to move his Indian Charity School from Connecticut to New Hampshire "for the education of Youth of the Indian Tribes, English Youth, and any others." Hanover's citizens offered Wheelock 3,000 acres of land, free labor, and cash to move his school to their town. Governor John Wentworth gave a royal charter to officially establish the school, and the Earl of Dartmouth in England made a generous donation. In gratitude, Wheelock named his college after the earl.

Dartmouth College and its town of 10,900 residents have since flourished. The college dominates both the town and region's economy and cultural life. Dartmouth itself boasts numerous beautiful buildings, including the famed Dartmouth Row on the east flank of the college green. These four Greek Revival buildings are the 1829 Wentworth Hall, Dartmouth Hall (a 1904 reproduction of the 1791 original destroyed by fire), Thornton Hall, and Reed Hall. The college's brick Webster Hall, fronted by tall columns, is named for Daniel Webster, its most famous alumnus. The 1928 Baker Memorial Library is modeled after Philadelphia's Independence Hall. In the library's basement is a spectacular, must-see series of frescoes called The Epic of American Civilization, painted by noted Mexican artist José Clemente Orozco in the early 1930s. The nearby **Hood Museum of Art** owns an interesting collection of African art, Assyrian bas-reliefs, and paintings by Italian, Dutch, and American artists.

The highway follows Main Street, leading right through Hanover to Dartmouth's campus before skirting around the quad on its east side. Stop and walk around the town and campus. Beside the classic buildings and museums are numerous bookstores, coffee shops, and interesting shops to browse through.

During Winter Carnival in February, fantastic ice sculptures cover the quad.

The Appalachian Trail, running 2,140 miles from Georgia to Maine, crosses the river and threads through Hanover before bending north and tackling the White Mountains. The New Hampshire portion of the trail totals 157 miles.

Hanover to Orford

Back on NH 10, the road edges around the east side of campus before heading north. The drive's next leg runs 17 miles from here to Orford along the terraced riverbank. Past the Hanover Country Club golf course is the Cold Regions Research and Engineering Laboratory, a US Army Corps of Engineers research center on glaciers and polar conditions. The flat road passes a few homes and businesses before leaving town and re-entering the countryside. A few miles upstream is **Hanover Boat Landing,** a popular put-in spot for canoeists. The generally wide and placid Connecticut River offers superb canoeing on its flat water. There are lots of canoe rental places, some offering shuttle service between put-ins and take-outs on the river. As the tar road rolls north, good views unfold of the green Vermont hills to the west.

Almost 10 miles from Hanover, the drive edges the east side of Lyme Hill and enters the village of **Lyme.** This rural farming community is dominated by the narrow town green and its whitewashed, wood-frame Lyme Congregational Church topped by a spire with a small octagonal dome. The church still has 27 numbered and painted horse stalls that were assigned in bygone days to Sunday parishioners. Nearby is a cemetery filled with old gravestones. The town, settled in 1761 and named for England's Lyme Regis, also offers the 1809 Lyme Inn and the excellent **Lyme Country Store.**

Past Lyme, the highway passes **Post Pond Preserve,** a town recreation area with good canoeing and fishing. The road then crosses a low gap and follows Clay Brook north onto the flat river

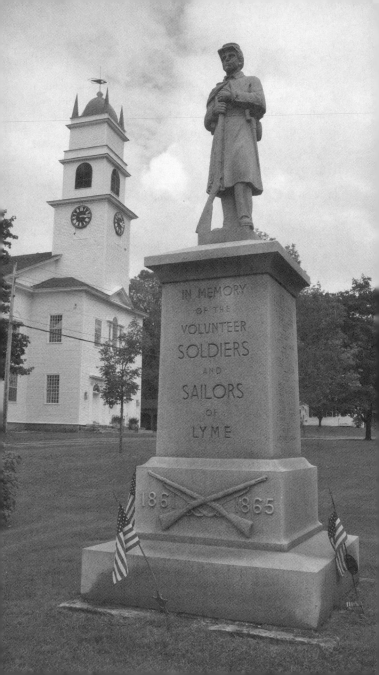

IN MEMORY
OF THE
VOLUNTEER
SOLDIERS
AND
SAILORS
OF
LYME

1861   1865

A schoolboy skateboards past the Lyme Country Store along the scenic route.

floodplain. Large cornfields and prosperous-looking farms with large barns spread across the fertile bottomland. The 132-foot-long **Edgell Bridge** crosses Clay Brook just west of the drive route. The bridge, built in 1885, was preconstructed on Lyme Common and transported to the bridge site for assembly—a precursor of modern prefabrication. Farther north is 64-acre **Reeds Marsh,** a state wildlife area that offers excellent birding on a swampy bend of the wide river.

A monument on the Lyme town green commemorates the sacrifice of soldiers and sailors who died in the Civil War.

Bright sunflowers provide a sunny backdrop to the idyllic "white picket fence."

Next the road gently turns northeast and enters the lovely old town of **Orford.** Set among green hills on the river's edge, Orford is one of those charming, unforgettable villages that travelers stumble across in rural New England. It boasts the **Orford Street Historic District,** a collection of stately white mansions dubbed Ridge Row, set back from the tree-lined highway. The houses, built in styles including Greek Revival and federal, were erected between 1773 and 1839 for wealthy businessmen and professionals. They perch in a long row along a low ridge east of the road, fronted by wide, manicured lawns. The town also contains two churches—the 1854 Victorian Congregational Church and the Universalist Church. In the town center is the all-purpose Weeks General Store, established in 1804, and the Orford Social Library.

The drive ends here in the town center where NH 25A crosses the river to Fairlee, Vermont, and I-91. Fairlee is dominated by the Fairlee Palisades, a series of sheer precipices that offer sport for rock climbers. From I-91, travelers can easily go north to St. Johnsbury or south to White River Junction.

2 Bristol–Rumney

General description: A 63-mile loop through scenic hills and valleys on the southern edge of the White Mountains.

Special attractions: Hebron Marsh Wildlife Sanctuary, Paradise Point Nature Center, Sculptured Rocks Natural Area, Newfound Lake, Wellington State Park, Sugar Hill State Forest, Cardigan State Park, Canaan Historic District, Lower Shaker Village, Rumney, Rumney Pound, Polar Caves, Mary Baker Eddy House, fishing, camping, swimming, rock climbing, wildlife observation, skiing.

Location: West-central New Hampshire.

Drive route numbers: US 4, NH 3A, 104, 118, and 25.

Travel season: Year-round.

Camping: No public campgrounds along drive.

Services: All services in Plymouth, Bristol, Danbury, Canaan, and Rumney.

Nearby attractions: Robert Frost Place, Sugar Hill Historical Museum, Polly's Pancake Parlor, Connecticut River Valley, Clark's Trading Post, Mount Washington, Conway Scenic Railroad, Echo Lake State Park, ski areas, Presidential Range Wilderness Area, Sandwich Range Wilderness Area, Pemigewasset Wilderness Area, Appalachian Trail, Madison Boulder Natural Area, White Lake State Park.

The Route

This 63-mile loop drive, beginning and ending in West Plymouth just west of Plymouth and I-93, traverses the unspoiled heartland of New Hampshire. Crossing rolling hills and following shallow valleys south of the White Mountains, the drive offers pleasant scenery, quiet back roads, a few quaint villages, and several backwoods natural areas.

Bristol–Rumney

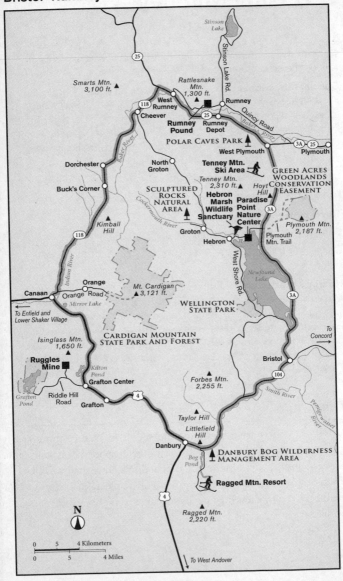

Stinson Lake

Stinson Lake Rd.

Smarts Mtn.
3,100 ft.

Rattlesnake
Mtn.
1,300 ft.

West
Rumney

Rumney

Cheever

Quincy Road

Baker River

Rumney
Pound

Rumney
Depot

Dorchester

North
Groton

POLAR CAVES PARK

West Plymouth

Plymouth

Tenney Mtn.
Ski Area

GREEN ACRES
WOODLANDS
CONSERVATION
EASEMENT

Buck's Corner

SCULPTURED
ROCKS
NATURAL
AREA

Tenney Mtn.
2,310 ft.

Hebron
Marsh
Wildlife
Sanctuary

Hoyt
Hill

Paradise
Point
Nature
Center

Plymouth Mtn.
2,187 ft.

Kimball
Hill

Cockermouth River

Groton

Hebron

Plymouth
Mtn. Trail

Indian River

Orange

Newfound
Lake

Canaan

Orange Road

Mt. Cardigan
3,121 ft.

West Shore Rd.

WELLINGTON
STATE PARK

To Enfield and
Lower Shaker Village

Mirror Lake

Isinglass Mtn.
1,650 ft.

CARDIGAN MOUNTAIN
STATE PARK AND FOREST

To
Concord

Ruggles
Mine

Kilton
Pond

Bristol

Grafton
Pond

Grafton Center

Forbes Mtn.
2,255 ft.

Smith River

Riddle Hill
Road

Grafton

Pemigewasset River

Taylor Hill

Littlefield
Hill

Danbury

DANBURY BOG WILDERNESS
MANAGEMENT AREA

Bog
Pond

Ragged Mtn. Resort

To West Andover

Ragged Mtn.
2,220 ft.

N

0   5   4 Kilometers

0   5   4 Miles

West Plymouth to Bristol

The drive begins in **West Plymouth,** reached by driving 4 miles west on New Hampshire 25/3A from Plymouth and exit 26 on I-93. Turn south on NH 3A at the rotary in West Plymouth. The town is a small collection of homes and a few businesses. The highway heads south through fields below the east flank of broad-shouldered, 2,310-foot Tenney Mountain and Tenney Mountain Ski Area. The road ascends gentle slopes and dips through shallow valley bottoms before climbing out of the flatland onto thickly for-ested hillsides. At 3.5 miles the road reaches a gap between Hoyt and Pike Hills and drops into a broad valley.

The highway reaches its junction with North Shore Road after 5 miles. Plymouth Mountain Trail begins off Pike Hill Road

A tree-lined side road leads to Rumney Town Pound, a stone enclosure used to pen stray livestock.

just east of the road and scales 2,187-foot **Plymouth Mountain** via a moderate 3.6-mile round-trip trail through lush woods. The north side of the mountain is protected by the Green Acres Woodlands Conservation Easement.

Turn west (right) on North Shore Road for a side trip to several interesting natural areas. A mile down the road is **Paradise Point Nature Center and Sanctuary,** a 43-acre preserve that encompasses 3,500 feet of the pristine northwest shore of Newfound Lake. A mature forest of white pine, red spruce, and eastern hemlock blankets the sanctuary, part of the Newfound Audubon Center. Paradise Point Nature Center, open through the summer months, is an educational facility operated by the Audubon Society with three interpretative trails that explore the surrounding woodlands and lakeshore. Tupelo trees, rarely seen in New England, are found on the Elwell Trail. On other trails are abundant hemlocks, some as old as 150 years, that are probably remnants of virgin forest. Most of the area's mature white pine and red spruce were cut long ago as prized timber, but two tall, straight white pines along the Swamp Trail are estimated to be at least 175 years old.

The nature center offers excellent birding opportunities, particularly along the lake edge. Mergansers, diving under the water for food, dot the lake, while a host of woodland birds, including dark-eyed juncos, pileated woodpeckers, northern waterthrushes, and golden-crowned kinglets are seen among the trees. The nature center offers interpretative programs, hands-on displays, and a bird-viewing area.

Another mile down North Shore Road at the head of Hebron Bay on the northwest corner of Newfound Lake is 34-acre **Hebron Marsh Wildlife Sanctuary,** part of the Newfound Audubon Center. This area includes open wetlands along the mouth of the Cockermouth River. Park at Ash Cottage just off the road and

A tall fountain graces the town green in Rumney, an old village first settled in 1765.

walk on a short trail through oak woods to the marsh. The edge of the marsh makes a great bird-watching vantage point. The swamp is an important stopover for migratory birds, including black ducks and mallards. Acute observers might also spot loons, grebes, ospreys, beavers, muskrats, and perhaps even a moose splashing through the marsh. This is also a good place to observe great blue herons as they gracefully hunt for small fish and frogs in the shallows.

A third point of interest on this side road lies a couple of miles farther west on Groton Road. Drive through the lovely village of Hebron with its whitewashed homes and two churches to Groton, then turn west off the main road to 272-acre **Sculptured Rocks Natural Area.** After driving another mile, park at a sign and step right to the Sculptured Rocks. Here the **Cockermouth River** chiseled under and through immense granite boulders that fill a narrow chasm, forming deep pools in immense potholes polished by swirling river water since the last ice age. A short trail meanders past small cascades and more pools among the mossy boulders. After visiting the rocks, retrace your steps back to NH 3A and turn south (right).

The highway hugs the eastern shore of 4,106-acre **Newfound Lake,** a pretty lake set amid high hills. Almost all the shoreline is developed, with numerous homes, cabins, motels, inns, businesses, and private beaches. After 6 miles the highway reaches West Shore Road at the very southern tip of the lake. This road runs northwest along the lake a few miles to **Wellington State Park and Beach.** This small parkland offers one of New Hampshire's finest inland sand beaches and the largest freshwater beach in the state's park system. It also has picnic facilities, canoeing (but no boat launch), fishing for bass and trout, and hiking trails. A developed boat launch abuts the beach.

Past the lake, the highway runs a mile down the broad Newfound River Valley and enters **Bristol,** a medium-sized town on the banks of the Pemigewasset River. A long business strip backed by houses flanks the road. Keep an eye out for the highway's Y

Summer cottages line the eastern shore of Newfound Lake, which is replenished twice a year by eight underwater springs.

junction with NH 104. Keep right at the junction and merge onto NH 104 for the next 9-mile segment of the drive.

Danbury, Grafton & Canaan

The highway leaves town and heads southwest, cresting a small rise then descending into the Smith River Valley. The road follows the slow, meandering river. Fields and blocks of forest lie along the asphalt. Low hills border the southern valley edge, while higher peaks, including 2,255-foot Forbes Mountain, block the northern horizon. The highway swings around Taylor Hill, crosses the river, climbs around Littlefield Hill, and passes the turn to **Ragged Mountain Resort** at 8 miles. On the western edge of long, thin Bog Pond is 246-acre Danbury Bog Wildlife Management Area. The ski area, with a 1,250-foot vertical drop, 45 trails, and 3 terrain parks, lies to the south on the northern slopes of 2,220-foot Ragged Mountain. It's only a 90-minute drive from Boston.

The drive crosses a low ridge and gently descends into **Danbury.** Its 1855 church, without a steeple, sits alongside the highway as it enters town. Go right on US 4 where it meets NH 104 at the village center. The next 14 miles travel northwest along the floor of the lovely valley of the Smith River. Low, undulating hills abut the U-shaped valley that was excavated and rounded by the ice sheet covering ancient New England. Old hill farms with cleared fields are scattered along the fertile bottomland beside the twisting river. At 5.8 miles the highway passes the East Grafton General Store. About 1.5 miles later it reaches Grafton and **Grafton Center.** The village's 1812 burying ground sits on the left just past the Congregational Church.

In Grafton Center, turn left at the Village Green on Riddle Hill Road for an interesting side trip to **Ruggles Mine.** Sitting on the south slope of Isinglass Mountain, the mine is a popular visitor attraction. Ruggles Mine opened in 1803 and is the oldest mica, feldspar, and beryl mine in the United States. More than 150 different minerals have been found here, including amethyst, rose and smoky quartz, and garnet. The open-pit mine has interpretive rooms and tunnels that illustrate the formation of the surrounding mountains as well as a gift shop. Mineral collecting is permitted with a paid admission ticket. Other old mica mines are scattered across the surrounding hills. Mica was once used for transparent windows, but today is used on electrical equipment.

West of the mine is **Grafton Pond,** a beautiful and unspoiled lake that is considered one of New Hampshire's best wildlife-viewing sites. Mammals seen here are moose, bear, otter, deer, and bear. The lake also hosts several nesting pairs of loons.

Back on the route, the highway leaves Grafton and skirts 68-acre **Kilton Pond,** a good fishing and canoeing lake. A large beaver lodge lies at the pond's marshy north end. The tar road crosses the lower east flank of Isinglass Mountain then passes Tewksbury Pond and shining Mirror Lake, headwaters of the Smith River, before entering the historic village of Canaan.

Canaan sits on the banks of the Indian River in a wide valley surrounded by hills. The old village, incorporated in 1761, is preserved today in the **Canaan Historic District.** Handsome old buildings and houses line the highway, once called Broad Street. The **Old Meeting House,** built in 1793 and listed on the National Register of Historic Places, still has its original bell clock. Nearby is the 1828 Old North Church built in Gothic Revival style. The **Canaan Historical Museum,** built in 1840 as an academy and one of the nation's first integrated schools, displays local history including medical equipment, handmade tools, and Shaker farm and household artifacts. The museum is open June through October on Saturday afternoons. Old houses, some dating from the 1790s, line the maple-bordered streets.

Take an interesting side trip from Canaan by journeying west a few miles to the **Lower Shaker Village** on Mascoma Lake. The Shakers, living in their own self-contained communities, were a Christian sect officially called The United Society of Believers in Christ's Second Appearing. During services the believers would enter trancelike stances to whirl and "shake" off sin and evil. The village here is one of New England's best-preserved Shaker villages, and was an active Shaker community between 1793 and 1923. Among the 13 buildings still on the site is the Great Stone Dwelling, the largest building ever constructed by Shakers, as well as the only remaining wooden Shaker cattle barn. Managed as a museum of Shaker life, the village also exhibits various artifacts, such as early sulfur matches invented by the Shakers, furniture, and wooden boxes. It also keeps Shaker songs, crafts, and gardening methods alive. The fee area is open mid-May through mid-October.

Canaan to Rumney

At Canaan, turn north (right) onto NH 118 for the next 15-mile drive section, which leads to West Rumney. About 0.5 mile out of town is the turnoff to **Cardigan State Park.** This 5,655-acre natural area encompasses 3,121-foot Mount Cardigan, a popular hiking destination. The trailhead is reached by driving east through Orange on narrow Orange Road and continuing on the dirt road to the trailhead for West Ridge Trail. The 3-mile trail climbs 1,300 feet to the mountain's bald summit. The mountain is a huge mass of erosion-resistant rock called Kinsman Quartz Monzonite, formed when a great pluton (mass of molten rock) slowly cooled underground. This rock crowns the summit and is well exposed on the peak's upper slopes.

Just above timberline, the summit is an island of alpine plants that are seen more often on the highest New England peaks or the farther north reaches of Canada. A fire lookout atop the mountain offers one of central New Hampshire's best and widest views. To the east and south spread low, wooded hills, while the ragged mass of the White Mountains looms on the northern horizon. To the west stretch the Connecticut River Valley and the rolling crest of the Green Mountains, the spine of Vermont. Abundant blueberries are found along the trail by hikers in August.

The main drive route heads north alongside the Indian River in a shallow, flat valley. The road slowly ascends past swamps and fields into rolling pine- and spruce-covered hills. Kimball Hill rises steeply to the east. After almost 7 miles the highway crests a ridge and good views spill north of the White Mountains, framed by the surrounding low hills. The road descends and crosses Bucks Brook before steeply rising again onto a shoulder of Streeter Mountain. Here the road begins a long descent through woods and across flattened terraces.

At **Cheever** is the pretty Cheever Union Chapel, a small white church with colorful stained glass windows. Below Cheever the drive steeply drops into the broad Baker River Valley. The highway ends at NH 25 just west of West Rumney. Turn east (right) on NH 25 toward West Plymouth for the last 9 miles of the drive.

NH 25 follows a bench along the south bank of the Baker River, a small, meandering river that marks the southern edge

The Newfound River dashes and tumbles over boulders at Bristol.

of the White Mountains. The road runs through small **West Rumney** and, after a couple of miles, reaches the **Nathan Clifford Memorial Rest Area,** with picnic tables and tourist information, on the left. Clifford, born near here in 1803, was a congressman, negotiated the Treaty of Guadalupe Hidalgo in 1848 to end the Mexican-American War, and was a Supreme Court justice from 1858 to 1881.

In 3 more miles the highway reaches Stinson Lake Road. Take a left here to Rumney. This historic village sits around a central town green. The metamorphic rock cliffs just west of here on the steep flanks of Rattlesnake Mountain are popular for their excellent rock-climbing opportunities, with hundreds of climbing routes on almost 20 different crags. Check out the climbing guide *Rock Climbing New England* for information on the area's climbing opportunities.

East of Rumney on Quincy Road is the unusual **Rumney Town Pound.** Most town pounds, used to enclose stray animals, were constructed of sturdy stone walls with a gate. The Rumney Pound used existing huge boulders to create the fence. These boulders are studded with small, delicate amethyst crystals. Also near Rumney, on Stinson Lake Road, is the **Mary Baker Eddy Home.** Eddy, founder of the Church of Christ, Scientist, lived here in the 1860s. The home is open for tours May through October.

The highway continues southeast past the **Polar Caves Park,** a popular attraction that includes a self-guided tour through chilly caves in the broken cliffs and boulder fields, a maple sugar museum, and other exhibits. The road heads down the broadening valley and, 3 miles from Rumney, enters West Plymouth where the drive ends. Travelers can continue east on NH 25 from the rotary to reach Plymouth and I-93.

3 Lake Winnipesaukee

General description: An 81-mile loop around the Ossipee Mountains and the north shores of Lake Winnipesaukee and Squam Lake.

Special attractions: Squam Lake Natural Science Center, Squam Lake, Center Sandwich, White Mountain National Forest, Hemenway State Forest, Mount Chocorua Scenic Area, White Lake State Park, Ossipee Mountains, Wentworth State Park, Lake Winnipesaukee, Castle in the Clouds, hiking, historic villages, fall foliage, picnicking, fishing, boating.

Location: Central New Hampshire.

Drive route numbers: NH 113, 113A, 16, 28, and 109.

Travel season: Year-round.

Camping: White Lake State Park offers 200 campsites, including 25 first-come, first-served sites. Many private campgrounds are found near Lake Winnipesaukee and Squam Lake.

Services: All services in Plymouth, Ashland, Holderness, Center Sandwich, West Ossipee, Center Ossipee, Ossipee, Wolfeboro, and Tuftonboro.

Nearby attractions: White Mountain National Forest, Sandwich Notch, Sandwich Range Wilderness Area, Madison Boulder Natural Area, Conway, North Conway, Kancamagus Highway, Mount Washington, Crawford Notch, Franconia Notch State Park.

The Route

The 81-mile Lake Winnipesaukee Scenic Route follows a series of highways and back roads through scenic country on the north shores of Squam Lake and Lake Winnipesaukee and around the Ossipee Mountains in central New Hampshire. The lakes are the glistening centerpieces of the lovely Lakes Country, a region of rolling hills dotted with 273 lakes and ponds, including 30 that are more than 100 acres in size. The largest, grandest, and most popular is sprawling Lake Winnipesaukee, New Hampshire's largest lake,

Lake Winnipesaukee

MAINE
NEW HAMPSHIRE

To Conway

Eaton Center

East Madison

Madison

Silver Lake

Silver Lake

Chocorua

Chocorua Lake

To Conway

Big Rock Cave Trail

Mt. Wonalancet
WHITE SANDWICH RANGE WILDERNESS AREA

Wonalancet

BIG PINES NATURAL AREA

HEMENWAY STATE FOREST

Whiteface

Durgin Bridge

MOUNTAIN NATIONAL FOREST

Sandwich Mtn.
3,993 ft.

Sandwich Notch

Sandwich Notch Rd.

Campton

WEST BRANCH PINE BARRENS PRESERVE

Ossipee Lake Rd.

Effingham Falls

Bennett Road

HEATH POND BOG NATURAL AREA

To Union

Gov. John Wentworth S.H.S.

WENTWORTH STATE PARK

Ossipee

Lake Wentworth

To Alton

Center Ossipee

Grant Peak 1,500 ft.

Bayle Mtn.

OSSIPEE MOUNTAINS

Canaan Mtn. 2,000 ft.

Mt. Shaw 2,600 ft.

Tuftonboro

Center Tuftonboro

Wolfeboro Center

Wolfeboro Falls

Wolfeboro

West Ossipee

South Tamworth

Johnson Mtn. 2,200 ft.

Mt. Roberts 2,600 ft.

Castle in the Clouds

New Road

Sodom Road

Center Sandwich

Sandwich

Bearcamp Pond

Berry Pond

Moultonborough

Melvin Village

Long Island

Lake Winnipesaukee

Rattlesnake Island

SQUAM MOUNTAINS

WEST RATTLESNAKE NATURAL AREA

Squam Lake

Center Harbor

Bear Island

Mt. Percival 2,235 ft.

Mt. Morgan

Mt. Livermore

Cotton Mtn.

Squam Lakes Natural Science Center

Holderness

Little Squam Lake

Meredith

Campton Campground

To Lincoln

Ashland

To Franklin

N

0 3 6 Kilometers

0 3 6 Miles

The gates are seldom closed on the back roads along the Lake Winnipesaukee Scenic Route.

covering 72 square miles with a convoluted 183-mile shoreline and 274 habitable islands. Squam Lake is considered by many to be New Hampshire's most beautiful lake with its forested islands, rocky shore, and stunning setting. The drive threads along the north and east shores of these two lakes and explores bucolic woodlands around the Ossipee Mountains. Open year-round, the route offers generally uncrowded roadways except for the busy stretch of NH 16 between Ossipee and Chocorua.

Along Squam Lake

The loop drive begins in Ashland just east of exit 24 on I-93. Leave the interstate and drive east a short distance into town, then turn north on US 3 and head toward Holderness. **Ashland,** with lots of visitor services, has the **Whipple Home Museum,** birthplace of the 1934 winner of the Nobel Prize for medicine, George Hoyt Whipple. The highway runs northeast of town through commercial strip development along the north shore of 408-acre

Little Squam Lake. A point of interest is the **Squam River Bridge,** a small covered bridge at the lake's west-side outlet. Built in 1990 by Milton Graton, the bridge is New Hampshire's newest covered bridge.

Just before the town of Holderness lies the **Squam Lakes Natural Science Center,** a 200-acre museum and wildlife sanctuary that interprets and explores New Hampshire's diverse native flora, fauna, and life zones. The center provides a 0.75-mile exhibit trail, Gordon Children's Center, field trips, lectures, and educational activities. The drive route turns north (left) on NH 113 in Holderness.

The next 12-mile segment of the drive section from here to Center Sandwich, winds along the north shoreline of **Squam Lake** past numerous summer cottages, then heads through pastures and dense woodlands below the southeastern slopes of the Squam Mountains. Quiet coves with anchored boats lie along Squam Lake's scalloped shoreline. Thick woods along the lower flanks of Cotton Mountain and Mount Livermore hem in the road. Squam Lake, covering 6,765 acres, is perhaps New Hampshire's loveliest lake. It is well known as the locale for the 1981 movie *On Golden Pond,* starring Henry Fonda and Katharine Hepburn. "The loons! The loons are welcoming us back!" cried Hepburn's character in the film. The loons are still here, nesting on small isolated islands undisturbed by motorboats. The lake is renowned for its fishing— for salmon and lake trout along with smallmouth bass, perch, pickerel, and smelt.

After almost 4 miles the highway passes Bennett Cove and swings north around the low rise of **West Rattlesnake Mountain.** A roadside pullout marks the trailhead for the 1.8-mile round-trip Old Bridle Path Trail. The easy path ascends 450 feet to the mountain's 1,260-foot summit and a spectacular view south across Squam Lake. Another good trail begins just around the corner. The Morgan–Percival Loop climbs 5.8 miles north to the summits of Mounts Morgan and Percival in the Squam Mountains.

The highway bends northeast and travels through dense woods of white pine, oak, maple, and birch. Occasional cleared fields framed by overgrown stone walls interrupt the forest. After 11 miles, passing a large, marshy beaver pond and an old cemetery, the highway makes a steep descent into the Red Hill River Valley and reaches its junction with NH 109 in Center Sandwich.

Center Sandwich to Chocorua

The village of **Center Sandwich** is one of those gorgeous New England villages often seen splashed across color postcards. This crossroads town is exceptionally well preserved with three churches, a small museum, and many lovely federal- and colonial-style homes dating from the early 19th century set on its tree-lined streets. The steepled First Baptist Church with a graveyard alongside is one of New Hampshire's best-looking churches. The **Sandwich Historical Society Museum,** housed in a shoemaker's 1850 home, displays kitchen and household implements and artifacts dating from the village's 18th-century birth. The **League of New Hampshire Craftsmen** arose in Center Sandwich at the Sandwich Home Industries, one of seven crafts shops run by the league. A stop here at their retail shop reveals the state's diverse crafts, including pottery, woven goods, furniture, woodwork, and jewelry. For an excellent side trip, head northwest from town on Grove Street, which climbs northwest to beautiful and remote Sandwich Notch.

To continue the drive, turn left on NH 113 in the town center and head northeast past the museum, town hall, and the Transportation Museum at the Quimby Barn. Past the village, the quiet back road enters hills covered with dark woods occasionally broken by cleared fields and stone walls. The road twists through a forest and 3.7 miles later reaches North Sandwich. Continue straight north on NH 113A where NH 113 turns east. The highway runs over more low hills, passing a few homes. **Mount Whiteface,** a 4,010-foot peak in the 35,800-acre Sandwich

Range Wilderness Area, looms to the north—white rocks crown its summit.

After a couple of miles, the road bends east and crosses Whiteface River, a pretty stream tumbling through a shallow rocky gorge. After 6.5 miles the highway leaves the woodland and enters a broad clearing flanked by high mountains. A lovely white church sits against the woods on the north side of the pasture in **Wonalancet,** a small rural village with a few houses tucked among the trees. A large farm occupies the clearing. Just past Wonalancet is the trailhead for Big Rock Cave Trail, a 1.6-mile trail that climbs over Mount Mexico en route to Big Rock Cave.

The highway bends south past a historic marker that details the Chinook Kennels, breeders of sled dogs used for numerous polar expeditions and explorations, and the Admiral Byrd Memorial "to all noble dogs whose lives were given on dog treks during the two expeditions to Little America, Antarctica." The asphalt winds through thick forest and past an old cemetery and, 10 miles from North Sandwich, reaches the Swift River. The road twists along the river's north bank and 0.5 mile later comes to the **Big Pines Natural Area** in **Hemenway State Forest.** The forest itself is a 2,106-acre reserve on the slopes of Great Hill southwest of the river. The 139-acre Big Pines Natural Area along the wild river protects a splendid grove of 150-year-old white pines, including one with a 42-inch diameter—one of New Hampshire's largest pines. Others exceed 150 feet in height.

The white pine, a magnificent straight tree, is one of New England's most beautiful and revered trees. The pine has long been important to the region's economy and history. White pine wood was often used by early colonists to build homes and furniture, and the British Royal Navy reserved all pines with diameters larger than 24 inches for use as masts and spars on ships. Towering pines shade the highway as it winds along the riverbank here.

After a few miles the road enters **Tamworth,** where it intersects NH 113. Tamworth is famed for the **Barnstormers Theater,** a summer theater group that has offered plays every summer since 1930. Turn east (left) on NH 113. The highway runs 2.6 miles northeast up a shallow valley on the north slope of Page Hill before descending gradually to Chocorua and NH 16. A mile north (left) on NH 16 is Chocorua Lake. The 222-acre lake perfectly reflects the bare, pointed summit of rocky 3,475-foot **Mount Chocorua,** a favorite subject of artists and painters. Birches and pines along the lakeshore frame this gorgeous view.

The peak, the second-most-climbed mountain in the state, is laced with trails. The Piper Trail, beginning a couple miles north of the lake, is the most popular summit route. The mountain is named for Chocorua, a 1760 Ossipee Indian chief who was killed near the summit after a feud with settlers.

Chocorua to Wolfeboro

The main drive route goes south (right) on NH 16 and passes through a thick commercial strip bordering the highway. After 1.4 miles the busy road leaves Chocorua and runs through gentle river bottomland. **White Lake State Park** is reached after 3 miles. The popular 577-acre parkland surrounds White Lake, a good canoeing and fishing pond with a fine beach area graced with exquisite sand and warm water. The park offers a 200-site campground open from May through mid-October. Besides the lake and its recreational opportunities, White Lake State Park also protects the **White Lake Pitch Pines,** an 80-acre National Natural Landmark on the northwestern shore of the lake. These old-growth pitch pines, relatively rare New Hampshire trees, grow tall and straight and give the air an aromatic, resinous scent on warm summer days. The fire-resistant pitch pines are more commonly seen on Cape Cod.

East of the highway and state park, off NH 41, is the 341-acre **West Branch Pine Barrens Preserve.** This unique area is populated by white, red, and pitch pines and scrub oaks on a well-drained sandy glacial outwash plain. The area, protected by The Nature Conservancy, is one of New England's best-preserved pine

barrens ecosystems. The 1.5-mile-long Pine Barrens Loop Trail makes an interesting and easy hike through this unique area.

Back on the drive, continue south through **West Ossipee** into swamplands along the Chocorua River for 14 miles to Ossipee. The highway runs below the east flank of the **Ossipee Mountains,** a lofty granite range ringed by volcanic dikes. Geologists say the range is one of the best examples of a ring dike complex. This formed when the crust here drifted over a hot spot that welled up from the Earth's mantle. Volcanic eruptions, including outpourings of ash and lava, covered the land. After the volcanic rock above was eroded away, the roots of the hot spot were left exposed.

A sign warns motorists that moose often cross the highway between the mountains and the lowlands to the east as the drive continues. After a few miles the highway runs through forest west of **Ossipee Lake,** a huge 3,092-acre lake that cannot be seen from the highway. Much of the lakeshore is rimmed by summer cottages and homes, except for the 400-acre Ossipee Lake and 6-acre Heath Pond Bog natural areas on the lake's south side. **Heath Pond Bog,** owned by the New Hampshire Division of Parks, is a superb example of a quaking sphagnum bog, while a 1994 report called the Ossipee Lake area "New Hampshire's most significant sandy pondshore ecosystem, including the largest collection in N.H. of rare plants among pondshores and basin marsh communities."

This distinctive ecological community, a designated National Natural Landmark, is accessed by a 0.5-mile loop trail that begins 2 miles east of Center Ossipee on NH 25. Heath Pond Bog lies in a kettle hole, a deep depression formed when a chunk of glacial ice was embedded in the surrounding glacial till. After the ice block melted, the resulting cavity filled with water and formed a pond. The plants both in and around the bog community remain

The classic Wonalancet Union Chapel is tucked among trees alongside the scenic route.

from a time when New England's climate was cooler. Trees surrounding the bog are mostly spruce and tamarack, both boreal species. The bog surface is dominated by sphagnum moss but also is home to other plants, including orchids, carnivorous pitcher and sundew plants, sedges, and laurel. Eventually the bog will fill with decayed vegetation, forming peat. Be prepared with bug spray for abundant blackflies and mosquitoes when hiking here in spring and summer.

The drive continues south from **Center Ossipee** on NH 16, passing a large glacial erratic boulder on the right before traversing a low ridge. The highway descends into a business area and, 14 miles from Chocorua, reaches its junction with NH 28. Turn west (right) on NH 28 toward Wolfeboro, 10 miles away.

The highway rolls over low hills, passing swamps and moose stomps along the roadside before dropping down to Willey Brook. At 7.4 miles the road reaches **Wolfeboro Center** and a junction with NH 109. **Wentworth State Park** lies on the north shore of Lake Wentworth just east of NH 28 on NH 109. The small 50-acre park offers a good swimming beach, picnic area, and bathhouses. Farther down NH 109 is the **Governor John Wentworth State Historical Site.** Here are the remains of the 1769 summer estate of the first of New Hampshire's royal governors. The house, now just a foundation, is considered by many to be the first summer vacation home built in America. The mansion was 100 feet long and 2 stories high. The keys to the front door weighed 1.5 pounds each. Manicured lawns with English-style gardens surrounded the house. During the Revolution Wentworth was exiled and became governor of Nova Scotia. This estate burned to the ground in 1820.

The main drive route continues southwest from Wolfeboro Center along the forested north shore of the lake; in a couple of miles, travelers enter Wolfeboro Falls and Wolfeboro. Sitting on

Mount Chocorua, the second-most-climbed mountain in New Hampshire, towers above Fowlers Mill Cemetery.

sheltered Wolfeboro Bay on the southeastern corner of Lake Winnipesaukee, **Wolfeboro** stakes its claim to being America's oldest summer resort town. The town arose after Governor Wentworth built his summerhouse on adjoining Lake Wentworth. By the early 1800s summer cottages began lining the shores of Lake Winnipesaukee at this village named in honor of British general James Wolfe, a French and Indian War hero. During the 19th century Wolfeboro flourished as a summer resort.

Not much has changed. Wolfeboro is still a premier summer destination, with lots of boating, fishing, and shopping. Numerous shops line the city streets. A good excursion here is a ride on the venerable **M/S Mount Washington** from Wolfeboro to Weirs Beach. The 230-foot-long boat, holding 1,250 passengers, cruises a 50-mile, 3-hour trip daily from late May into October. The original *Mount Washington,* which burned in 1939, operated from 1888 to 1939. Historic points of interest in Wolfeboro include the 1778 **Clark House Museum** complex operated by the Wolfeboro Historical Society, with an 1868 schoolhouse and the replica of a 19th-century firehouse, and the Wright Museum of American Enterprise.

Along Lake Winnipesaukee

In Wolfeboro's business area is the junction of NH 28 and NH 109. Turn north (right) on NH 109 at the Civil War Memorial and village green. The road heads northeast past an old cemetery, homes, and businesses. A few miles out of town the highway passes the **Libby Museum.** The museum's collection, exploring the area's history and natural history, includes a 350-year-old dugout canoe, Abenaki Indian artifacts that date back almost 7,000 years, and artifacts found at the site of Governor Wentworth's nearby 18th-century summer home. The highway continues up the northeast side of Lake Winnipesaukee past numerous homes and summer cottages.

New Hampshire's largest body of water, **Lake Winnipesaukee** was, like most of New England's geographic features, formed by glaciation. When the great ice sheets crept across the land here, they scooped out an immense depression in this region of poor granite. Deposits of boulders left by the glacier at the southern end of the lake impeded drainage and allowed water to accumulate in the hollow, forming today's huge lake. Lake Winnipesaukee, covering 44,586 acres, is an irregular patchwork with a 183-mile shoreline, quiet coves and harbors, jutting forest-clad peninsulas, and 274 habitable islands.

The highway dips and rolls along the wooded lakeshore, with occasional glimpses of blue water glistening in the sun. Just past the highway's intersection with NH 109A is **Melvin Village,** a charming town perched on the north edge of Melvin Bay. The high, wooden Abenaki Tower yields great views of the lake and its many islands. The highway continues northwest and, a few miles later, joins NH 171.

A good side trip tracks east down NH 171 to **Castle in the Clouds.** This famed mansion at the end of a narrow, one-way, 1.8-mile road perches on a hilltop above Lake Winnipesaukee. The castle was built in 1913 by shoe mogul Thomas Plant on his 6,000-acre estate on the lake's shores and the southern flank of the Ossipee Mountains. Plant brought more than 1,100 Italian stonecutters and masons to build the castle, which he called Lucknow. The place included uncommon conveniences for that time—an intercom, self-cleaning oven, central vacuum, and a clothes-drying system. Its eclectic architecture was influenced by Japanese, Swiss, Norwegian, Norman, and English architectural styles. The mansion, completed in 1914, cost more than $7 million. Plant, after some sour investments, died destitute in 1941.

Later the house was bought by Richard Robie and eventually opened to the public. Today visitors can tour the castle, ride horses or walk on more than 45 miles of trail, and sample the famous Castle Springs water. Views from the castle grounds are well worth the entry fee alone. Below spreads the crystal-clear lake dotted with green islands and surrounded by wooded hills and mountains.

Back on the main route, the highway runs west from its junction with NH 171 to NH 25. Turn left at the intersection with NH 25 and jog 0.5 mile before turning northwest again on NH 109 in Moultonborough. The drive's last 5 miles run northwest to Center Sandwich. The road passes marsh-edged Berry Pond and moves along through cleared fields lined with stone walls. Thick woods flank the asphalt. After 3 miles the highway dashes through **Sandwich,** a lovely small village with spacious old homes spread over the rounded top of Wentworth Hill. The highway drops steeply down the hill, passes an old burying ground, and a couple of miles later enters Center Sandwich and the drive's terminus at a junction with NH 113. Go left on NH 113 to head back to I-93 and Ashland, the drive's start.

4 Kancamagus Highway

General description: A 58-mile paved highway that traverses the scenic heart of the White Mountains between Bath and Conway in northern New Hampshire.

Special attractions: Swiftwater Falls, Swiftwater Covered Bridge, White Mountain National Forest, Kinsman Notch, Lost River Reservation, Agassiz Basin, Sabbaday Falls, Rocky Gorge Scenic Area, Lower Falls Scenic Area, Swift River, hiking, backpacking, camping, fall foliage, rock climbing, swimming, picnicking, scenic views.

Location: North-central New Hampshire.

Drive route number: NH 112.

Travel season: Year-round. Expect possible snow and winter driving conditions between November and April.

Camping: 7 national forest campgrounds—Big Rock (28 sites), Blackberry Crossing (26 sites), Covered Bridge (49 sites), Hancock (56 sites), Jigger Johnson (76 sites), Passaconaway (33 sites), and Wildwood (26 sites)—with drinking water, tables, toilet facilities, and fireplaces are found along the drive. The campgrounds are open from late April to mid-October. Other national forest campgrounds are located within easy driving distance. Camping is available at Dry River Campground in Crawford Notch State Park (36 sites) and Lafayette Place Campground in Franconia Notch State Park (98 sites). Many private campgrounds are found in the White Mountains.

Services: All services in Conway, North Conway, Lincoln, and Bath.

Nearby attractions: Franconia Notch State Park, Robert Frost Place, Sugar Hill Historical Museum, Connecticut River Valley, Clark's Trading Post, Mount Washington, Conway Scenic Railroad, Crawford Notch State Park, Echo Lake State Park, ski areas, Presidential Range Wilderness Area, Sandwich Range Wilderness Area, Pemigewasset Wilderness Area, Appalachian Trail, Madison Boulder Natural Area, White Lake State Park.

Kancamagus Highway

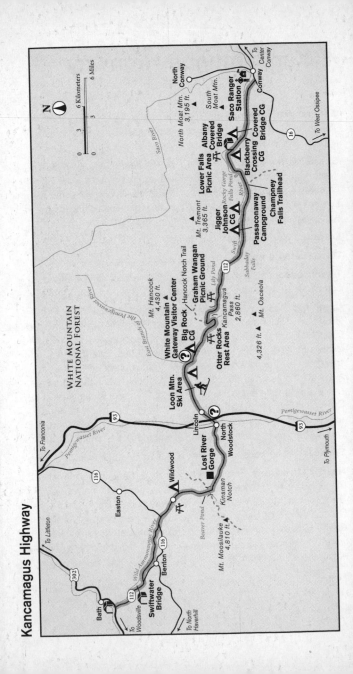

The Route

The **White Mountains,** encompassing northern New Hampshire, form a brooding highland creased with glacier-carved valleys broken by abrupt granite outcrops lorded over by knobby peaks. The range, including almost 50 peaks above 4,000 feet, was named by early sailors off the Maine coast who saw glistening white snowfields on the highest summits on clear spring days. The Whites, with 86 separate peaks and 9 notches (passes), are divided into 3 subranges—the Presidential, Carter-Moriah, and Franconia ranges. These rumpled mountains, dark with woodlands, are often wreathed in clouds that swirl through amphitheaters and cirques. Capricious weather, characterized by high winds, rules these lovely, savage hills.

The dominant force that shapes the White Mountains and the lives that intermingle with them is climate. The range straddles an area where two storm tracks meet. Frigid masses of dry, subpolar air, sweeping down from the north and west, converge with warm, moist air pumped north from the subtropics and the Caribbean. This clash of weather systems brings a volatile mix of heavy rain and snow, sudden thaws, hard freezes, and quick temperature reversals that determines what plants and trees cling to these hills, which animals inhabit its forests, and how its human occupants cope with such weather vagaries.

The highest summits in the White Mountains experience extreme weather conditions and temperatures as well as some of the most powerful winds on the planet. On the summit of 6,288-foot Mount Washington, the range's high point, the thermometer regularly plunges below zero degrees Fahrenheit and the mountain hides behind clouds 55 percent of the time. Wind gusts over 100 miles per hour have been recorded in every month. The second highest wind was reported here on an April day in 1934 when the weather observatory atop Mount Washington's summit recorded one gust at an astounding 231 miles per hour. Another record is the 49.3 inches of snow that fell at the station during a

The Swift River runs alongside the Kancamagus Highway in the heart of the scenic White Mountains.

24-hour period in February 1969. That 2-day storm deposited a whopping 98 inches of snow on the summit.

The Kancamagus Highway Scenic Route traverses the heart of the White Mountains, and is one of New England's premier drives. Following NH 112 for 58 miles, the drive runs from the Ammonoosuc River near Woodsville on New Hampshire's western border to Conway just west of the Maine boundary. In 1989 a 28-mile highway stretch between Lincoln and Conway became the **Kancamagus Highway,** one of the nation's first designated National Forest Scenic Byways. Until the late 1950s only two dead-end roads, one on each side of Kancamagus Pass, pointed at each other through the thick woods. Earlier trails were hacked out of the wilderness by settlers who built small farms on the fertile land along the Swift River west of Conway. With the advent of automobiles, the idea of a transmountain highway slowly grew. The land was surveyed in the 1930s, but the road wasn't completed until 1959. In 1964 the highway was paved, and it opened to year-round traffic in 1968. Today, more than one million vehicles traverse the highway annually.

The two-lane, paved highway has numerous scenic pullouts. Watch for heavy traffic, particularly in the busy summer months and in autumn when hordes of leaf-peepers descend on the White Mountains to view the fall foliage. The Kancamagus is considered one of New England's premier foliage drives. Take your time and use the turnouts to view the scenery. The first drive section over Kinsman Notch is usually less traveled.

Expect variable weather along the byway. Snow can fall anytime between October and May, although the spring months are typically rainy. Summers are pleasant and balmy, with daily highs occasionally reaching into the 90s. Autumn days are usually perfect, with warm days and cool nights. Rainy spells that last for several days do occur. Winters are cold and snowy. Expect icy and snowpacked road conditions and plan accordingly.

Over Kinsman Notch to Lincoln

The drive description begins 3 miles east of Woodsville at the junction of US 302 and NH 112. This start is easily accessed from I-91 in Vermont. Take exit 17 and head east through Wells River and Woodsville to NH 112. Otherwise, begin the drive from I-93 at exit 32 in Lincoln or from Conway on the east at the intersection of NH 112 and 16.

The drive starts at the quiet highway junction of US 302 and NH 112 at the confluence of the **Wild Ammonoosuc** and **Ammonoosuc Rivers** near their larger junction with the Connecticut River in Woodsville. The Ammonoosuc, an Abenaki Indian word for "wide fishing place," originates at the Lake of the Clouds southwest of Mount Washington's summit. The rock-strewn river grows and tumbles almost 6,000 feet from its headwaters down to the Connecticut River. The first drive segment runs 21 miles from here to Lincoln via Kinsman Notch.

The highway heads southeast following the south bank of the Wild Ammonoosuc River, a tributary of the Ammonoosuc River, through low wooded hills. Tall white pines and hemlock abut the asphalt. Turn left at 2.2 miles to the 174-foot-long **Swiftwater Bridge,** an 1849 covered bridge spanning the Wild Ammonoosuc. At Swiftwater Falls the river rushes over rocky benches below the bridge, forming a picturesque scene and pleasant summer swimming hole. Park at a small lot on the north side of the bridge to access the river. Just past the bridge, the road enters the hamlet of **Swiftwater,** undoubtedly named for the frothy river, with a few homes and a general store. Past town, the drive plunges through thick woods punctuated by orderly Christmas tree farms and, after almost 7 miles, enters **White Mountain National Forest.**

Covering most of northern New Hampshire, the national forest protects 784,505 acres in New Hampshire and Maine—a larger land area than the state of Rhode Island. The forest, the largest single piece of public land in New England, lies within a day's drive of more than a quarter of the US population and, as such, is an exceedingly popular recreation area. It covers more than 11 percent of New Hampshire, the highest percentage of federal land in any eastern state. Six designated wilderness areas in the national forest, including both New Hampshire and Maine, total 149,432 acres.

The forest was established after the lumber industry denuded the mountainsides of trees during the late 19th century. Many organizations, including the Appalachian Mountain Club and the Society for the Protection of New Hampshire Forests, joined with state governor Frank Rollins and US Representative John Weeks for the passage of the Weeks Act of 1911. The act enabled the federal government to establish the national forest and protect its valuable watersheds and timberlands by buying back private property east of the Mississippi River.

The highway continues alongside the river, passing a junction with NH 116 at 10 miles. This is, historically, a great spot for moose sightings. In the 19th century, guests at Franconia-area inns would ride carriages to this intersection to be rewarded with evening moose viewings. Wildwood Campground and recreation area is reached at 12 miles. The campground offers 26 shaded campsites along the river.

Here the road bends south and begins climbing. Marvelous views of 4,810-foot **Mount Moosilauke,** the first grand mountain in the range, and its satellite peaks unfold through the windshield. Mount Moosilauke was first ascended in 1773, and offers a superb summit reached via the Appalachian Trail from Kinsman Notch. This beautiful trail section is a natural garden of wildflowers lined by waterfalls. As the highway climbs, roadside rock changes from the metamorphic Littleton Schist to the harder Kinsman Quartz Monzonite, a type of granitic rock. This well-exposed rock is a coarse-grained, gray rock flecked with gleaming bits of black biotite and white feldspar crystals. The road passes a small cascade and picturesque Beaver Pond with its single pine-clad island before reaching the summit of **Kinsman Notch** after almost 15 miles.

The notch was named after early settler and farmer Asa Kinsman who, with his wife, took the wrong track en route to their new home at Landaff in the 1780s. Instead of turning around, the pair hacked a new trail over this wild pass, which now commemorates their labor. The first road came through the notch in 1916. Beaver Brook Trail, part of the white-blazed Appalachian Trail, begins at the top of the notch. The trail climbs southwest to the summit of Mount Moosilauke along Beaver Brook, littered with flowers all summer, and after 0.33 mile reaches the start of a delightful chain of cascades. Continue up the trail past a dozen tumbling cascades in the steep ravine. Watch for many slick rocks while hiking alongside this steep section.

From the notch the highway bends east and drops down the sharp valley of the Lost River. About 0.5 mile down is **Lost River Gorge and Boulder Caves,** one of the most popular scenic attractions in the White Mountains. The 152-acre reservation, a preserve operated by the Society for the Protection of New

Hampshire Forests, is a labyrinth of moss-covered boulders where the Lost River appears and disappears beneath the jumbled rocks. The gorge was formed, like most of New England's features, by glaciation. Some 15,000 years ago a great ice sheet crept over the mountains, excavating the notch and rounding the deep valleys. Later, as the climate warmed, the ice on the notch's north side lasted longer and drained its meltwater down the Lost River side. The frothy torrent sharply incised the gorge out of hard granite. The maze of boulders tumbled from the cliffs above, filling the gorge for today's sightseers. The Lost River Trail, beginning near the gift shop, explores the gorge and its tunnels on a system of walkways and stairs. Paradise Falls, a 20-foot waterfall, is near the base of the gorge. Lost River Gorge, a fee area, is open from mid-May to mid-October.

The drive drops 6 miles and 900 feet from Kinsman Notch down a widening valley to Lincoln. About 2 miles from the pass, the road leaves the national forest. Farther east is a junction with scenic NH 118. The lower part of the valley is called Agassiz Basin for Louis Agassiz, a Swiss geologist who was one of the first scientists to recognize that great ice sheets once covered North America and Europe. Evidence found here helped confirm his theories.

The highway continues east in the flattening valley alongside the Lost River as it riffles over bedrock and boulders. After 20 miles the road enters North Woodstock, crosses the Pemigewasset River, and passes exit 32 on I-93 to reach Lincoln. At the southern gateway of Franconia Notch in the broad Pemigewasset Valley, **Lincoln** is an old town that was named in 1764 for the Earl of Lincoln. This tourist town offers numerous facilities and services, including many accommodations and restaurants. Nearby is the **North Woodstock–Clark's Trading Post Covered Bridge.** The 75-ton, 120-foot railroad bridge, originally built in Vermont, was taken apart and reassembled over the Pemigewasset River.

Up to Kancamagus Pass

The second section of this route runs 37 miles from Lincoln to Conway over the famed **Kancamagus Highway.** The highway is named for Kancamagus, a native Abenaki Indian who was chief of the Penacook Confederacy of 17 tribes in the late 1600s. Passaconaway, his grandfather, united the tribes in 1627. Kancamagus worked in vain to keep a fragile peace between the tribes and the English settlers moving into their valleys, but after being slighted by the colonial government, he gave in to the more inflamed factions and led several raids on the settlers. The 1689 raid on Dover was particularly brutal. The colonists began a protracted campaign of retaliation that forced Kancamagus to disappear with his tribe into Canada.

A couple of miles past the interstate, NH 112 leaves Lincoln and heads east into White Mountain National Forest along the **East Branch of the Pemigewasset River. Loon Mountain Ski Resort** scatters across the slopes of 3,073-foot Loon Mountain, to the south. The area offers a year-round gondola ride that yields impressive views and access to a nature trail atop the mountain. An informational kiosk, detailing the forest and its facilities, sits by the roadside another mile up the highway. Farther along is 56-site **Hancock Campground,** a popular camp spot for trout anglers, in a lovely birch forest on the river's north shore.

The **White Mountain Visitor Center** lies just north of the highway on the east side of the bridge over the river. Stop in for maps and information on the forest. It's also the trailhead for the popular **Lincoln Woods Trail,** which heads north along an old railroad bed beside the East Branch River into the Pemigewasset Wilderness Area, a trail noted for its logging relics and splendid waterfalls.

At the bridge over the East Branch, 5 miles from Lincoln, the highway bends southeast and follows the Hancock Branch. The asphalt gently ascends the valley, which closes in. Three lofty peaks—West Peak, Mount Osceola, and East Peak—loom to the south above wooded slopes. **Big Rock Campground** has 28 riverside sites. **Upper Lady's Bath,** a swimming hole, is a 5-minute walk from the campground.

At 7 miles is Otter Rocks Rest Area, with picnic tables and river access. Hancock Notch Trail begins another 2.4 miles up the road. Here the highway makes a hairpin turn and begins laboriously climbing out of the valley. **Pemi Overlook,** just past the second switchback, offers great views down the glacier-carved valley to the west and north to Mount Hitchcock and Mount Hancock with its obvious glaciated cirque. A mixed woodland of balsam fir, red spruce, and birch borders the highway.

Past the overlook, the highway steepens to an 8 percent grade and climbs almost 3 more miles to the summit of 2,860-foot **Kancamagus Pass.** A parking lot, viewpoint, and the **C. L. Graham Wangan Ground Picnic Area** sit just east of the pass summit. The picnic ground is the site of an ancient American Indian celebration. Stop here and take in the view. Marvelous vistas of the White Mountains surround this height-of-land. To the east stretches the wide, wooded Swift River Intervale, and to the north sprawl the 45,000-acre Pemigewasset and 27,380-acre Presidential Range–Dry River wilderness areas. The mountains are composed of hard, erosion-resistant Conway granite, a coarse, pink granite laced with pegmatite dikes.

The highway begins dropping east off the summit down a 7 percent grade. After a few miles it swings past elegant Lily Pond, a small lake surrounded by tall grass. Lily Pond is part of the Swift River's headwaters. The road, passing Sawyer River Trailhead and Sugar Hill Overlook, begins to flatten out 5 miles from the top of the pass. The overlook yields excellent views down the valley with the sharp edge of Greens Cliff and Owl Cliff to the northeast. Pointed 3,475-foot Mount Chocorua fills the southeast horizon. Farther along is the Sabbaday Falls parking area on the south side of the highway.

Sabbaday Falls to Conway

Park and take a short 15-minute hike south to one of the White Mountains' prettiest and most famous waterfalls. The trail runs south alongside Sabbaday Brook through open forest. **Sabbaday Falls** is a series of three drops that funnel down a narrow gorge chiseled into soft basaltic dikes that were intruded into the harder Conway bedrock. The first drop tumbles into a large basin; the creek then roars through a chute and pours down a 25-foot cliff into a deep chasm filled with spray, moss, and thundering white-water. The trail leads to a crystalline pool at the base of the chasm before climbing a fenced walkway to a point above the falls. The trail is very popular in summer and autumn, so be prepared for company. Also remember that no bathing or swimming is allowed in the brook or waterfall area.

Sabbaday Falls were named, so the story goes, by early settlers who first came upon the frothy cascade on a Sunday or Sabbath. They returned every succeeding Sunday, their day off from work, to view the falls and picnic. They called it the "Sabbath Day" trip, which eventually became Sabbaday.

The drive continues east on the south side of the **Swift River** through second-growth forests punctuated by occasional clearings and moose stomps. This whole area was almost denuded by loggers in the late 19th century. The Swift River Railroad, running 20 miles up the valley from Conway, was completed in 1906 and brought wholesale decimation to the area's virgin forests. In 1912 forest fires and floods swept across the valley. The establishment of the White Mountain National Forest a few years later halted the clear-cut tactics of the lumber industry and allowed the forest to grow again. Today's Kancamagus Highway follows much of the old railroad grade along the Swift River.

The highway passes several trailheads, and 3 miles from the falls reaches the **Russell-Colbath House,** an 1830s cabin staffed with guides in period clothes. The cabin offers information and displays on area nature and history. Thomas Russell built the

small, wood-frame house in 1832 on a 2,000-acre homestead along the Swift River and ran a nearby sawmill. His son Amzi inherited the home and in turn passed it on to his daughter Ruth in 1887, the only one of his children who had not moved away.

Ruth lived here with her husband, a carpenter named Thomas Colbath, until one windy autumn day in 1891. Colbath went out for a walk, telling Ruth, "I'll be back in a little while." He didn't return in a little while, so she kept his supper warm and lit a kerosene lamp in the kitchen window. Colbath's "little while" turned out to be 42 years. During that entire time the faithful Ruth placed the lamp in the window every evening. Nicknamed the "hermit woman," she maintained her vigil until her death at age 81 in 1930. A newspaper wrote of her: "No other woman in America leads such a lonely life during the bleak winters that shut in the valley of Passaconaway as this dear old lady of solitude." Her estate—land, house, and personal property—was sold. Tom Colbath returned 3 years later after wandering through Cuba, South America, and California and tried to obtain possession of the house. His claim was denied and he disappeared.

The house, listed on the National Register of Historic Places, is operated by the Forest Service and open to tours in the warmer months. Take note of the hops vines outside the cabin. Almost every rural New England homemaker had her own recipe for beer as well as bread, making the cultivation of these vines especially important.

Nearby is 76-site **Jigger Johnson Campground** and the **Rail and River Trail.** This short hiking loop explores the area's trees and shrubs, including balsam fir, white pine, mountain maple, and black cherry. Bear Notch Road, beginning just past the campground, runs north 9 miles through scenic Bear Notch to Bartlett. It makes a good bike tour with gentle grades up, a steep but short grade down, and little competing traffic.

Sabbaday Falls, reached by a short trail, thunders over bedrock into a narrow chasm filled with spray and moss.

Back on the highway, continue east along the south bank of the Swift River. The **Champney Falls trailhead** is on the right a mile down. It's only worth hiking the 1.5-mile trail during high-water season or after heavy rains; otherwise, the falls are meager. **Rocky Gorge Scenic Area** is reached after 3 more miles. Here the Swift River, dropping 10 feet over a ledge, slices down through bedrock granite to form an abrupt, narrow gorge. Swimming is prohibited in the Rocky Gorge area since currents here are treacherous and powerful. *Reader's Digest* magazine in 1949 reported the amazing story of a woman who attempted to wade the river above the falls and was swept downstream. She was found alive hours later, dangling upside down in an air pocket under the falls by an ankle wedged in the bedrock. A short path meanders down to the river and falls from the parking area and crosses the river on a footbridge. Continue a short distance to **Falls Pond,** a charming tarn below Bear Mountain. Look for carnivorous pitcher plants along the swampy shoreline in summer. The area forest includes mountain maple, paper birch, sugar maple, red oak, mountain alder, and shadblow, a shrub covered with white blossoms in May. The Rocky Gorge Scenic Area also offers picnic tables, restrooms, and drinking water.

The highway bends northeast past Rocky Gorge and runs above rapids in the rock-strewn river. The Rainbow Slabs and Painted Walls, both good climbing crags, stretch along the hillside north of the Swift River. The river's **Lower Falls** are a couple of miles from the Upper Falls at Rocky Gorge. This is another spectacular display of whitewater, particularly during heavy spring runoff when the river surges over bedrock ledges and boulders. During summer's low water the area teems with swimmers and sunbathers who jam the rocks and parking lots. The **Moat Mountains** dominate the skyline northeast of here. The mountain massif is the erosional remnant of an immense blanket of volcanic

The Swift River drops 10 feet over polished granite benches at Rocky Gorge Scenic Area alongside the Kancamagus Scenic Route.

The sturdy 136-foot-long Albany Covered Bridge offers great views of the Swift River and the White Mountains.

rock that covered New Hampshire during long episodes of volcanism some 175 million years ago.

At Lower Falls the highway turns south and passes a picnic area, 26-site Blackberry Crossing Campground, 49-site Covered Bridge Campground, and **Albany Covered Bridge** over the Swift River. This 136-foot span, dating from 1858, is of the Paddleford Truss design with graceful interior-arch trusses. The 2.5-mile Boulder Loop Trail leaves from Covered Bridge Campground and yields sweeping views of the Swift River Intervale and rocky, 3,475-foot Mount Chocorua, an isolated and spectacular peak named for a Pequawket Indian chief who was killed on its slopes.

The last 6 miles of the drive continue east along the Swift River. The road runs through woods, with occasional glimpses of the river and the mountains beyond. It leaves the White Mountain National Forest and passes the Saco Ranger Station, a good information stop with a visitor center, before dead-ending at NH 16 on the southern outskirts of Conway. Turn left to go into **Conway** and **North Conway.** The twin towns, settled in 1764, form the southern gateway to the White Mountains. They were named for Englishman Henry Seymour Conway. A historic artists' colony and resort, the town of Conway attracts visitors with more than 200 factory outlet shops, as well as numerous other shops and restaurants. Nearby is Echo Lake State Park, several ski areas, and Whitehorse and Cathedral Ledges, the best climbing cliffs in New England. Conway and North Conway offer all visitor services.

5 Crawford & Franconia Notches

General description: A 55-mile scenic route through Crawford and Franconia Notches in the White Mountains.

Special attractions: Franconia Notch State Park, Profile Lake, The Flume, The Basin, Crawford Notch State Park, Arethusa Falls, Mount Washington Hotel, Appalachian Trail, Cannon Mountain, Cannon Mountain Ski Resort and Tramway, downhill and cross-country skiing, hiking, rock climbing, ice climbing, fishing, camping.

Location: Northern New Hampshire.

Drive route numbers: US 302 and 3, I-93.

Travel season: Year-round. Expect possible snow and winter driving conditions between November and April.

Camping: 2 national forest campgrounds are found on the drive: Zealand (10 sites) and Sugarloaf 1 and 2 (60 sites). Other national forest campgrounds are located within easy driving distance on the Kancamagus Highway. Camping is available in Crawford Notch State Park (36 sites) and Franconia Notch State Park (98 sites). Many private campgrounds are also found in the White Mountains.

Services: All services in Conway, North Conway, Glen, and Lincoln.

Nearby attractions: Robert Frost Place, Sugar Hill Historical Museum, Polly's Pancake Parlor, Connecticut River Valley, Clark's Trading Post, Mount Washington, Conway Scenic Railroad, Echo Lake State Park, ski areas, Presidential Range Wilderness Area, Sandwich Range Wilderness Area, Pemigewasset Wilderness Area, Appalachian Trail, Madison Boulder Natural Area, White Lake State Park.

The Route

This 55-mile drive begins in Glen, climbs over Crawford Notch, and swings around the mountains to spectacular Franconia Notch.

Crawford & Franconia Notches

Crawford & Franconia Notches

The grand Mount Washington Hotel has the entire Presidential Range, including Mount Washington, at its back door.

The drive traverses some of New England's best and most famous scenery in the notches, including Arethusa Falls, New Hampshire's highest waterfall. The White Mountains, stretching across northern New Hampshire, form a rough corduroy of rolling mountains and deep glacier-carved valleys. New England's highest range, the White Mountains are topped by 6,288-foot Mount Washington. Although people from the West consider these mere hills (even California transplant Robert Frost said, "The only fault I find with New Hampshire is that her mountains aren't quite high enough"), they remain the highest points east of the Black Hills and north of the Great Smoky Mountains.

The White Mountains tower almost 5,000 feet above the surrounding hills and are high enough that early sailors off the coast of Maine were amazed to see their snow-clad summits glistening in the sun. Florentine navigator Giovanni da Verrazano wrote to the king of France in 1524 of "high mountains back inland, growing smaller toward the sea." And in 1628 Christopher Levett recalled "a great mountain called the Christall hill, being as they say one hundred miles in the country, yet it is to be seen at the sea side, and there is no ship arrives in New England, either to the West so farre as Cape Cod, or to the East so farre as Monhiggen, but they see this mountaine the first land, if the weather be cleere."

The drive follows three highways—US 302, US 3, and I-93—between Glen and Lincoln. The paved roads are open year-round, although drivers should expect winter driving conditions with icy and snowpacked roads during the colder months. The highways can be very busy on summer and autumn weekends. Autumn, a wonderful time to drive this byway, brings a spectacular display of color to the roadside, making the route one of New Hampshire's best foliage tours. A good loop drive from either Conway or Lincoln combines this scenic route with the Kancamagus Highway drive for a full day's adventure.

Glen & Bartlett

Begin the drive in **Glen** at the junction of US 302 and NH 16, about 5 miles north of North Conway's commercial strip. Lying on the east side of the Mount Washington valley, Conway and North Conway form the eastern gateway to the White Mountains. Both are popular tourist towns, with bumper-to-bumper traffic along US 302/NH 16 and dozens of factory outlet shops that lure bargain hunters. Besides shopping, there's plenty to do and see in the valley. The **Conway Scenic Railroad** leaves from the 1874 North Conway Depot, offering a glimpse into the area's railroad past as it chugs along the Saco River. **Echo Lake State Park,** on the western edge of the valley, encompasses Echo Lake and **Cathedral and White Horse Ledges.** These two cliffs rising above the quilted valley offer some of New England's best rock-climbing adventures on their granite flanks. North of Glen on NH 16 is Pinkham North and the Mount Washington toll road. The Conway area also offers excellent and diverse downhill and cross-country skiing in winter.

In Glen, from the intersection of US 302 and north–south NH 16, go straight on US 302. Glen is a small tourist village with a strip of motels and services along the highway. The road crosses the Ellis River on the west side of Glen and then the Rocky Branch a mile later. Past here, the highway bends south past Bartlett Covered Bridge (now a gift shop), a 167-foot span over the Saco River, before crossing to the river's south bank. White's Ledge, a slabby granite outcrop, lies on the north side of the valley. **Attitash Mountain Resort,** one of the East's best ski mountains, sits farther west on the north slopes of Attitash Mountain. The resort offers a vertical drop of 1,750 feet, with 73 trails mostly geared to advanced intermediate skiers and massive snowmaking capabilities. In summer it has an alpine slide (the longest in North America) and a chairlift to an observation tower with a grand view of the Whites. On the north side of the road, just before the ski area, is the Fields of Attitash, a well-known equestrian center with regular summer competitions.

The residential hamlet of **Bartlett** sits 2 miles up the road. Bear Notch Road, beginning in the middle of town, makes a good side trip. The 9-mile road winds steeply south to scenic Bear Notch and drops gently to the Kancamagus Highway. After leaving the village the drive heads west alongside the Saco River up a textbook-example, U-shaped glacial valley. Looming mountains blanketed with a dense hardwood forest press in on the road. Their barren summits often scrape against sodden, gray clouds. These peaks form the southern end of the 15-mile-long Presidential Range, a major range in the White Mountains properly described by author Nathaniel Hawthorne as "majestic, and even awful, when contemplated in a proper mood, yet by their breadth of base and the long ridges which support them, give the idea of immense bulk rather than of towering height."

Mount Washington

Mount Washington, lying north of the Saco Valley, is the Whites' high point at 6,288 feet. It is also New England's most famous mountain. The broad peak, which includes New England's largest above-timberline ecosystem, was called Agiocochook by American Indians, a term loosely translated as "home of the Great Spirit." The Indians did not climb the sacred peak, so the first recorded ascent was by Darby Field in 1642. Hoping to find precious stones on the mountain, Field brought back a handful of diamonds that turned out to be quartz crystals. Today thousands of visitors reach the summit via a toll road, cog railroad, mountain bike, or foot. On the rare clear day, all of New England can be seen from this lofty perch.

The peak and range are famed for extreme weather conditions. Brutal combinations of wind and cold coupled with unsettled storm tracks give Mount Washington and the surrounding peaks the dubious distinction of having the world's worst recorded weather. The observatory atop the peak noted the second highest wind gust ever recorded on earth, 231 miles an hour, on a windy April day in 1934 (the highest recorded wind is 253 mph in 2010 at Barrow Island, Australia). Gusts above 100 miles per hour have been recorded every month of the year, and the average wind speed on the summit is 35 miles per hour. Snowfall averages 195 inches annually, with the average year-round temperature a frigid 26.9 degrees. Needless to say, area hikers need to be prepared for weather extremes and be skilled in the use of map and compass—and self-rescue.

Over Crawford Notch

Almost 9 miles from Glen, the highway enters White Mountain National Forest, the largest parcel of public land in New England, and passes Sawyer Rock Picnic Area. The road and valley gently bend to the northwest toward **Crawford Notch,** one of the most storied passes in New England. The notch was discovered accidentally in 1771 by Timothy Nash, a hunter tracking a moose. He climbed a tree to scout the way ahead and saw the dramatic notch that divides the Ammonoosuc and Saco Rivers. Since a good north–south route was needed to link new settlements in the northern Connecticut River Valley with southern New

Hampshire, Nash reported his discovery to Governor John Wentworth. The governor skeptically offered Nash a tract of land in the notch if he could bring a horse through it and present the undamaged animal at Portsmouth. Nash took the challenge and, with the help of a friend, succeeded in transporting the horse through the rugged gap and delivering it. A block-and-tackle was used to lower the obliging animal over several cliffs en route. Nash received his grant, and the trail through Crawford Notch quickly gained traffic. It became a state turnpike in 1803, the precursor of today's US 302.

The pass was named for Abel Crawford, an early entrepreneur who capitalized on tourism. Crawford and his son Ethan Allen Crawford blazed the Crawford Path in 1819, the first trail to the summit of Mount Washington; worked as tour guides; and established inns to accommodate visitors. Part of the Crawford Path, the 3 miles between the highway and Mount Clinton, comprise the oldest continuously maintained trail in the United States. The Crawfords settled here in 1792 and established Crawford House, the first hotel in the notch, in 1800. This famed hotel, in various incarnations, operated until 1977 when fire destroyed it.

The highway gently ascends the broad valley toward the notch. At 14 miles it passes **Frankenstein Cliff,** a tall crag named for George Frankenstein, an Ohio landscape painter. Major icefalls, attracting ice climbers, cascade down the cliff in winter. The Arethusa Falls trailhead is on the left at 14.7 miles. The 1.3-mile trail climbs 750 feet to secluded 176-foot **Arethusa Falls,** the tallest waterfall in New Hampshire. Coliseum Falls and Bemis Brook Falls, both small pretty waterfalls, are also along the trail.

Crawford Notch State Park's boundary lies at the trailhead. This 5,775-acre reserve is a 1.5-mile strip that runs up the valley floor to the crest of the notch. The park's 36-site **Dry River Campground** is just up-valley. The Appalachian Trail crosses

The short trek from Crawford Notch to the top of Elephant Rock rewards hikers with one of the best views in the White Mountains.

the highway at mile 17. A mile past the trail is the **Willey House Historic Site,** the location of one of the White Mountains' worst tragedies. The event, commemorated by a plaque on the house, occurred on Monday, August 28, 1826. Sam Willey, his wife, and five children, living in this lonely valley, were gripped in a torrential thunderstorm that raised the Saco River's level 24 feet in one night. They heard the terrible roar of a rock and mud avalanche loosened from the slopes above and ran, along with two hired men, for a nearby shelter but never made it. The slide struck a large boulder a scant 50 yards from the house and separated, sparing the frame building but burying the fleeing Willeys. A traveler stopped by several days later and found the dog barking and the house empty, but with a glass of toddy on a counter and Bible opened to the 18th Psalm—"Then the earth shook and trembled; the foundations also of the hills moved and were shaken." Three of the children's bodies were never recovered.

The aftermath of the fierce storm was described by Lucy Crawford, who wrote, "The whole valley, which was once covered with beautiful green grass, was now a complete quagmire, exhibiting nothing but ruins of the mountains, heaps of timber, large rocks, sand, and gravel. All was dismal and desolate." The slide area is still visible on the large rock slab and called, appropriately, Willey's Slide. The Willey House area makes a good road stop with marvelous views of the valley and surrounding mountains. The dam across the highway from the Willey House was used as a movie set one dreary November day for the New England film *Where the Rivers Flow North.*

Back on the drive route, the highway continues ascending northward toward the gap. Its asphalt is flanked by several 4,000-foot peaks, including Mount Tom, Mount Field, and Mount Avalon on the south and the slabby Webster Brook Cliffs on the north. **Mount Willard,** a 2,786-foot peak, dominates the windshield view. The 800-foot southeast face, one of the tallest rock faces in New England, offers excellent rock climbs in summer and climbs up ice-choked gullies in winter. On the opposite valley wall is Silver Cascade, a silvery streak of water that tumbles almost 1,000 feet down the steep flank of Mount Webster. The road climbs steeply below the rock face, and after a total of 20 miles, the drive reaches the gap of Crawford Notch, an abrupt pass framed by cliffs and called the Gate of the Notch.

Crawford Notch is the most famous and most spectacular of all the White Mountains' notches. Like most of New England's geographic features, the pass was formed by glaciation. Immense valley glaciers squeezed through the narrow notch opening and down into the valley. Later the ice thickened and overrode the surrounding mountains, including Mount Willard to the south of the gap. The mountain's north slope was gently smoothed by the passing glacier, but the cliffed southeast flank overlooking the valley was formed by the ice freezing against the granite and plucking the rock away as the ice passed.

Abel Crawford's inn at the notch was visited by numerous dignitaries, including Presidents Pierce, Grant, Hayes, Garfield, and Harding. Novelist Nathaniel Hawthorne, who often wrote about the White Mountains, noted that the hotel was "the pleasure house of fashionable tourists and the homely inn of country travelers." The hotel burned several times and was rebuilt until the last fire in 1977. Still standing in the notch, however, is the old Victorian train station where guests arrived. The station, the Crawford Notch Depot Visitor Center, is now an Appalachian Mountain Club (AMC) information center with advice on trails and hiking, and hot drinks during foliage season.

The top of the notch is considered the headwaters of the **Saco River,** which gathers in tiny Saco Lake before cascading southeast into the valley. The west side of the notch is drained by Crawford Brook, an upper tributary of the Ammonoosuc River. A fine hike from the notch follows a 0.25-mile trail to the rounded top of **Elephant Rock,** an aptly named cliff on the north side of the gap. Another good trail gently ascends an old carriage road for 1.4 miles to the summit of **Mount Willard.** The AMC hiking guide notes, "From perhaps no other point in the mountains can so

grand a view be obtained with so little effort." More intrepid hikers can tackle the trail along the crest of the Presidential Range, climbing 10 peaks en route, on long summer days. Begin by following the Crawford Path up Mount Clinton.

To reach the **Mount Washington Cog Railway,** follow the Mount Clinton Road around the western edge of the Presidential Range to the base station. The spectacular railroad, the first cog railroad in the world, was completed in 1869. Coal-fired steam engines push passenger cars up 3.5 miles of track with an average grade of 25 percent. One steep stretch, called Jacob's Ladder, rises 37.41 percent, or more than 1 foot in 3. At this steep section the passengers in the front of the car are 16 feet higher than those in the rear.

Crawford Notch to I-93

Past the notch, the highway drops northwest down a broad valley floored by sparkling Crawford Brook. This road stretch is notorious for moose-caused accidents. Be alert for animals crossing the highway, especially in the evening. As the road flattens away from the gap, the entire 15-mile Presidential Range stretches along the eastern horizon—Mounts Jackson, Clinton, Eisenhower, Monroe, Washington, Jefferson, Adams, Quincy Adams, and Madison. A low ridge of mountains borders the drive on the west.

The **Mount Washington Hotel,** a huge twin-turreted inn, is reached 4 miles from the notch. This genteel hostelry, with its white stucco facade, red-tiled roof, Doric columns, and 900-foot-long veranda, is a renowned and luxurious resort set amid forested hills below looming Mount Washington itself. Built by railroad baron Joseph Stickney, the hotel was the last great resort put up in northern New Hampshire and the only one still operating. It opened in 1902 after Italian craftsmen spent two years on

High above Crawford Notch, a rock climber inches up the nearly sheer noutheast face of Mount Willard.

its construction. The hotel's moment of fame, however, came in 1944 when the US government reserved the entire hotel for the Bretton Woods Conference, which would shape world economics in the post–World War II period. Representatives from the United States and 43 other countries met here and established the gold standard at $35 an ounce, made plans for the World Bank, and selected the dollar as the unit of international exchange. The hotel flourishes today as a three-season destination resort. It offers two golf courses, indoor and outdoor pools, tennis courts, horseback riding, and fishing.

Past the hotel, the highway runs through the small village of **Fabyan.** The cog railroad station can also be reached by turning right here on a marked road and driving east for 5 miles. The **Mount Washington Resort Bretton Woods,** New Hampshire's largest ski area, is also here, with 102 trails, a 1,500-foot vertical drop, 4 terrain parks, and night skiing on weekends. The area offers mostly beginner and intermediate slopes. A short distance away is a cross-country center with 100 kilometers of groomed trails.

The highway joins the **Ammonoosuc River** here and bends west down a broad valley. The river's name is an Abenaki Indian word for "wide fishing place." The river has long been a popular stream for anglers—among them Ethan Allen Crawford, who pulled out hundreds of pounds of trout and salmon to feed hungry guests. Just past Fabyan are the Lower Falls of the Ammonoosuc River. Here the river, forming a picturesque scene, slides over granite ledges. A short path, beginning at the large parking lot on the north side of the road, leads to the cascade.

Zealand Recreation Area includes a 10-site forest campground along the south bank of the river. Follow Zealand Road south past Sugarloaf Campgrounds 1 and 2 (60 sites), a lovely, secluded area by the Zealand River, and on to road's end where the **Zealand Trail** begins. The trail makes a good afternoon hike to two waterfalls and spectacular Zealand Notch. It heads south 2.7 miles to Zealand Falls and 4.8 miles to **Thoreau Falls,** a long cascade over rocky benches that was named for naturalist Henry

David Thoreau. This area was devastated by uncontrolled logging, then forest fires, and is only now being reborn.

Back on the main route, the drive reaches the junction of US 302 and US 3, the Daniel Webster Highway, in the village of Twin Mountain. Turn left on US 3 for the next 9 miles of the drive. The road enters White Mountain National Forest again, passes 7.3-acre **Beaver Brook Falls Natural Area,** a popular roadside area with a waterfall, and reaches the Mount Cleveland Scenic Vista after almost 7 miles. The view overlooks Beaver Brook and 2,397-foot Mount Cleveland to the northwest. The highway continues southwest, skirting the forested edge of the mountains. At 9.5 miles the drive reaches exit 36 on I-93. Continue straight for another mile and enter the southbound interstate lanes.

Franconia Notch

The last drive segment, running 11 miles from here to Lincoln, travels through Franconia Notch. Protected in a 6,692-acre state park, the notch offers breathtaking scenery and was home to New Hampshire's most famous landmark—the Old Man of the Mountain. Other natural features include The Flume, a deep stream gorge; The Basin, a glacial runoff–carved pothole; and Cannon Cliff, New England's tallest cliff. The interstate, here the Franconia Notch Parkway, narrows to two lanes as it zips down the valley. Several exits and parking areas give access to the area's special scenery.

Franconia Notch is a deep, narrow, 8-mile-long valley flanked by the lofty Franconia Range on the east and the Kinsman Range on the west. Several peaks over 4,000 feet high cluster in these two ranges, making them the lofty goals of many peakbaggers. Mount Lafayette, the 5,249-foot high point of the Franconia Range, was named in 1825 for the famed French general, the Marquis de Lafayette. The Pemigewasset River, originating at Echo Lake in the notch, dashes south along the valley floor.

Cannon Cliff, New England's tallest cliff, rises high above Franconia Notch and the scenic route.

The notch began as an ancient river valley some 60 million years ago. Later the land rose and the valley became deeply incised into the granite bedrock until glaciers began sculpting the land 60,000 years ago by carving out the U-shaped valley and forming abrupt cliffs on the mountain slopes.

The drive heads south on the interstate and in a mile enters **Franconia Notch State Park** at the notch itself. Echo Lake nestles in a hollow alongside the highway. Exit from the highway here and park. **Artist's Bluff,** a rounded rock dome north of the lake, gives a sweeping view of the lake, Cannon Mountain Ski Resort, and the glacier-carved valley to the south. A short trail climbs to the rock summit. In June, look for rare, protected white lady's slipper flowers here. The lake, reflecting the surrounding mountains, makes a good place to picnic, fish, boat, and swim.

The Basin, one of Franconia Notch's most beautiful wonders, features a lovely waterfall that tumbles into a sculpted glacial pothole.

An 8-mile, tar bike path, bordering the interstate from Echo Lake down to The Flume, makes a fun and scenic way to explore the notch.

Although only 4,040 feet high, **Cannon Mountain** in the Kinsman Range dominates the western skyline. The bulky mountain is named for an oblong pile of immense boulders on its shoulders that resembles a cannon as seen from the highway. A tramway here ascends 2,022 vertical feet in 6 minutes, climbing from the lake to the summit for a marvelous panoramic view of Franconia Notch, five surrounding states, and Canada on a clear day. The tram operates in ski season and from mid-May to mid-October. **Cannon Mountain Ski Resort,** the largest ski mountain in New Hampshire, offers 72 trails on a 2,180-foot vertical drop. The **New England Ski Museum,** displaying old skis, bindings, boots, ski clothing, and trophies dating from the late 1800s, sits near the foot of the tramway.

Old Man of the Mountain

At the far end of Echo Lake, a highway exit leads to a side road that drops south to the Profile Lake parking area and the **Old Man of the Mountain.** The Old Man, composed of five granite ledges that strikingly resembled a craggy human face in profile, was New England's natural version of Mount Rushmore until it fell into the cloudy night of May 3, 2003. The face, however, long inspired reverence in visitors with his jutting brow, sharp nose, pursed lips, and pointy-bearded chin. The 45-foot-high silhouette, poised 1,200 feet above Profile Lake on the brink of Cannon Cliff, not only looked human with its fine sculptural detailing and chiseled good looks, but also conveyed the flinty character of the classic New Hampshire Yankee.

The craggy Old Man of the Mountain, symbol of New Hampshire, fell apart during a stormy May night in 2003.

The Old Man was immortalized in Nathaniel Hawthorne's short story "The Great Stone Face" when he wrote "all the features were noble, and the expression was at once grand and sweet, as if it were the glow of a vast warm heart, that embraced all mankind in its affection, and had room for more." Not everyone, however, waxed poetic at his visage. Swedish writer Frederika Bremer said the face "resembles an old man in bad humor and with a night cap on his head, who is looking out from the mountains, half inquisitive."

The Old Man remained unnoticed until 1805 when Luke Brooks and Francis Whitcomb, two surveyors plotting a road through Franconia Notch, saw the profile after stopping to wash up in Profile Lake. Earlier Native American residents had no records of the rock face, although one legend says they saw the features of the Great Spirit in it and the right to view it was reserved only for their chiefs. The face, seen only from a few vantage points near the lake, was a huge tourist attraction in the 19th century. A railroad stopped at the Profile House, an impressive 400-room hotel on the lake's edge. Circus-man P. T. Barnum was so impressed with the Old Man that he wanted, tongue-in-cheek, to buy him for his show. The area was bought by the state and preserved as a natural area in 1927. The Old Man became the official emblem of New Hampshire in 1946.

The delicate formation, basically composed of several balanced, overhanging blocks of granite weighing more than 7,200 tons, was long considered unstable and subject to erosion by New Hampshire's severe climate. Geologists, as early as 1872 when a Boston newspaper reported the Old Man's instability, considered ways to forestall erosion's consequences and to secure the blocks to the main cliff. In 1916 a series of tie-rods and turnbuckles were first installed on the Old Man's forehead. Over the ensuing years more rods and cables were installed and caretakers sealed cracks and fractures with epoxy and resin atop the head to minimize the infiltration of water, which levers out the granite blocks through repeated freeze-thaw cycles.

All efforts, however, were in vain. Sometime on the foggy night of May 3, 2003, the Old Man of the Mountain fell. State park official Mike Pelchat told reporters the next day, "We always thought it was the hand of God holding him up, and he let go." Geologist Brian Fowler and New Hampshire state geologist David R. Wunsch analyzed the collapse and determined "that the same geological processes that created the Old Man ultimately led to his demise. . . . Tenacious chemical weathering, frost-wedging, mechanical stress, and gravity all have conspired to send the Old Man down to the talus pile below." While the state mourned the loss of its "Great Stone Face," Governor Craig Benson formed a task force to determine if the face could be rebuilt or if a replica should be sculpted near Profile Lake. The Old Man of the Mountain Revitalization Task Force eventually recommended a sculpture-lined path around Profile Lake, a museum at the base of Cannon Mountain, and a life-size replica of the Old Man. Ground was broken in 2010 for the first phase of the Old Man of the Mountain Memorial.

Past Profile Lake, the highway heads down a deep, wide gorge alongside the **Pemigewasset River.** Pemigewasset is an Abenaki Indian word for "swift current." The interstate highway through here, called the **Franconia Notch Parkway,** was the scene of a long standoff between development engineers and local environmentalists. The engineers wanted to continue the four-lane superhighway through the valley with shoulders and a wide median to accommodate high-speed traffic. Compromise was finally reached, and the result was today's excellent and scenic highway with two lanes, no passing, no left turns, and good access to the notch's wonders—the only such stretch of interstate highway in the nation.

As the highway descends, the towering eastern wall of Cannon Mountain hems in the valley on the west. The huge, vertical **Cannon Cliff,** reaching heights of 1,000 feet, is New England's tallest cliff. The 320-acre talus slope below the wall is the largest such area in New Hampshire. The cliff offers numerous rock-climbing adventures, ranging from short practice routes along the base to daylong affairs. Cannon Cliff was first climbed in 1928 via the Old Cannon route near the Old Man. Access to the crag is by trail from the Boise Rock parking area, named for woodsman Thomas Boise. Caught in a blinding blizzard at this overhanging boulder, Boise killed and skinned his horse to save himself, wrapping the warm, bloody hide around his body so that it encased him like a cocoon. The next day rescuers hacked him out of the frozen hide.

Lafayette Campground, with 98 sites, lies along the riverbank farther along. A pleasant 1-mile hike up to Lonesome Lake on the southern shoulders of Cannon Mountain takes off from the campground.

The Basin, 3 miles south of Profile Lake, is a beautiful glacial feature below a large, marked parking area on the west side of the highway. This unusual geologic formation was created over the last 25,000 years as torrential runoff from melting glaciers spun through a circular basinlike cavity in the granite bedrock. The river funnels down a narrow chute and plunges into a deep, clear pool polished by tumbling cobbles and boulders. Below the pool the water funnels through narrow channels. Overhung by cliffs on its upstream side, The Basin is 30 feet in diameter and 15 feet deep at its center. An excellent hike follows the Basin-Cascade Trail up Cascade Brook west of The Basin. Numerous beautiful cascades, Kinsman Falls, and lovely Rocky Glen Falls are along the first mile.

This area also harbors a rare old-growth white pine forest, a remnant of forest untouched by the axe. One hardy specimen straddling the creek towers 100-plus feet with a trunk exceeding 4 feet in diameter. The pine, between 300 and 400 years old, predates the American colonies. At that time every pine more than 2 feet in diameter and 72 feet tall was claimed, cut, and stamped with a crown for the Royal Navy as a "mast pine." The trail continues past Rocky Glen Falls another 1.4 miles to pretty Lonesome Lake in a cirque on the south slopes of Cannon Mountain.

The Flume, the last attraction in the notch, is reached a mile below The Basin. Exit the parkway and follow signs to the state park's Flume Gorge Visitor Center. The center, detailing the area's natural history with displays and a video show, makes a good introductory stop before visiting The Flume. Take the 5-minute bus ride or walk the 0.7-mile distance to the site. The Flume is a fee area. Buy a ticket at the visitor center. A good 2.1-mile loop hike begins at the center and explores The Flume and The Pool.

The Flume is a spectacular fissure that stretches 800 feet through the lower slopes of Mount Liberty. The gorge ranges from 12 to 20 feet wide with vertical moss-coated walls rising 90 feet above frothy Flume Brook. This cool, refrigerated canyon (temperatures are usually 15 degrees cooler than outside) is accessed by trails and a boardwalk. A longtime tourist favorite, The Flume was discovered in 1808 by a 93-year-old woman who was trout fishing near her homestead. The canyon was excavated by the stream, swollen with glacial snowmelt, as it ran along a soft basalt dike intruded into the more erosion-resistant Conway granite. The dike erodes much more quickly than the surrounding bedrock, resulting in the narrow, abrupt gorge.

Avalanche Falls, a 45-foot waterfall, sits at the head of The Flume. Atop the gorge, the trail threads northwest through woods to Liberty Gorge Cascade and another 0.1 mile to The Pool. This gorgeous spot on the Pemigewasset River is tucked into an immense basin 150 feet in diameter and 40 feet deep, surrounded by polished granite walls. The trail crosses a narrow covered bridge spanning the chasm, offering long views of The Pool and the valley. A grand, lone white pine once stood as guardian on a viewpoint above the pool, giving the name Sentinel Pine Point to the overlook. The path continues another 0.5 mile south to return to the visitor center. July hikers should keep an eye out for patches of delicious blueberries.

Back on the drive, continue south by getting back onto I-93 or heading down parallel US 3. Either way the drive quickly leaves the state park and enters the tourist strip development of North

Woodstock and Lincoln. The valley widens, and in a couple of miles, the drive ends at the junction of the interstate and NH 112, the Kancamagus Highway. A white colonial-style visitor information center sits at that intersection. Travelers have numerous choices from here. The interstate continues south to southern New Hampshire and its cities, while the Kancamagus Highway scenic drive heads east to Conway.

6 Upper White Mountains

General description: An 89-mile drive through deep glacier-carved valleys along the winding Androscoggin River, and through Dixville Notch in northern New Hampshire's White Mountains.

Special attractions: White Mountain National Forest, Pondicherry Wildlife Refuge, Moose Brook State Park, Weeks State Park, Androscoggin River, Dixville Notch State Park, The Balsams Hotel, Balsams Wilderness Ski Area, Colebrook State Park, hiking, backpacking, fishing, camping.

Location: Northern New Hampshire.

Drive route numbers and names: US 2, US 3, NH 110, 110A, 16, and 26, North Road, Grange Road, Lost Nation Road.

Travel season: Year-round. Expect possible snow and winter driving conditions between November and April.

Camping: Moose Brook State Park (59 sites) is near the drive's start at Gorham. Coleman State Park (25 sites) is north of NH 26 west of Dixville Notch. Several private campgrounds lie along the drive.

Services: All services in Gorham, Jefferson, Groveton, Errol, and Colebrook.

Nearby attractions: Robert Frost Place, Sugar Hill Historical Museum, Connecticut River Valley, Mount Washington, Conway Scenic Railroad, Echo Lake State Park, ski areas, Presidential Range Wilderness Area, Appalachian Trail, Franconia Notch State Park.

The Route

This 89-mile-long drive follows a series of highways and back roads that thread through the upper White Mountains in northern New Hampshire. This mountainous area, north of the popular Presidential Range of the White Mountains, traverses a remote, untrampled section of New England far from the outlet shops and tourist traps. The region is a high, brooding upland broken by rumpled

Upper White Mountains

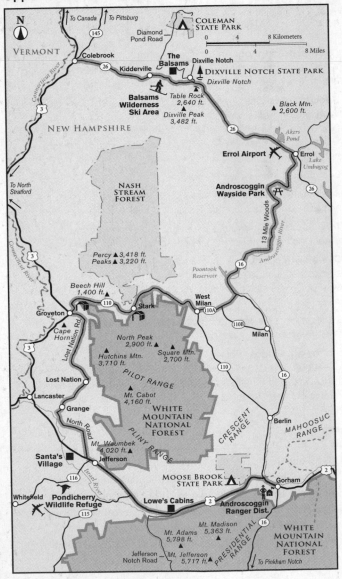

mountains and sliced by deep, glacier-carved valleys. Dense woodlands, interrupted only by occasional granite cliffs, blanket the hillsides. Travelers can expect excellent fall colors as well as frequent sightings of wildlife, especially moose, at dawn and dusk during autumn and spring. The year-round drive follows paved highways except for a narrow section between Jefferson and Groveton.

Gorham to Jefferson

The drive starts in **Gorham** at the junction of US 2 and NH 16. This intersection is easily reached via scenic Pinkham Notch from Conway on NH 16. Gorham, in a breathtaking setting, is a working-class village for paper mill employees. The town straddles the south bank of the Androscoggin River where it bends east to Maine. Settled in 1771, Gorham flourished after the railroad came in 1851 and made it the jumping-off place for White Mountain tourists. The old **Victorian Railway Station** on the town common is now a local museum that displays the area's railroad heritage. The Chamber of Commerce offers evening moose tours through the summer and early fall. A district ranger office in town has information and maps for White Mountain National Forest.

To begin the drive, head west on US 2 for 1 mile to the highway's junction with NH 16 north in Upper Village. Turn west on US 2. The highway heads west up the valley of the Moose River and, after a mile, reaches the turnoff to 87-acre **Moose Brook State Park.** This area offers a pleasant 59-site campground, a swimming pool, and access to good stream fishing. The park makes a good base for hikers to explore the Presidential Range to the south and the Appalachian Trail in the Mahoosuc Range to the northeast.

Past the park turnoff, the highway climbs steeply up Gorham Hill, flattens out, and reaches a scenic roadside view of the lofty Presidential Range to the south. Peaks seen from here include Mount Madison, Mount Quincy Adams, Mount Adams, and Mount Washington, the 6,288-foot high point of the White

Mountains. **Mount Washington,** the highest peak in the Northeast, was a sacred place called Agiocochook or "place of the Storm Spirit" by American Indians. Darby Field made the first recorded ascent in 1642 and brought back a handful of "diamonds," which turned out to be quartz crystals. The summit is renowned for some of the world's worst weather, including a world record 231-mile-per-hour wind gust in 1934.

Past the viewpoint, the highway drops west into the wide glaciated **Moose River Valley,** passing numerous trailheads that lead south into the Presidential Range. The scenery beyond the asphalt is simply spectacular, with some of New Hampshire's best offerings. The Crescent and Pliny Ranges hem in the valley to the north with high, forested mountains. The rugged profile of the Presidential Range dominates the southern horizon. The road crests a low divide near Lowe's Cabins and begins following the upper waters of the Israel River, a west-flowing tributary of the Connecticut River. The highway slowly angles northwest along the northern fringe of the hilly valley, with vistas of Franconia Notch and the Franconia Range unfolding to the southwest.

After 12.5 miles the highway reaches its intersection with NH 115. A few miles down this road is the excellent **Pondicherry Wildlife Refuge,** part of the **Silvio Conte National Fish and Wildlife Refuge,** a nature preserve designated a National Natural Landmark. The refuge, with more than 6,000 acres covered with dense woods around ponds, bogs, and streams, offers superb animal habitat for moose, beaver, otter, mink, deer, muskrat, fox, and coyote. Over 230 bird species also live here, including green-winged teal and ring-necked ducks, both rarely seen in New Hampshire.

The drive route descends through a secluded residential area and skirts the southern edge of the Pliny Range, topped by 4,020-foot Mount Waumbek, then passes the Starr King Cemetery. In summers past, the Waumbek theater was considered de rigueur for those seeking fine summer entertainment. Farther along is the Jefferson Historical Society Museum, housed in an 1869 church, and a scenic viewpoint with two picnic tables. The town of Jefferson is just past this point.

Jefferson is an unadorned village perched on open slopes above the Israel River Valley. Superb views from this town often lure travelers from below the notches in autumn. Jefferson is named for the author of the Declaration of Independence and second US president. It was settled in 1772, incorporated in 1796, and since then has been a popular summer community. Look for local maple syrup for sale here in early spring. Splendid stands of sugar maple drape the hills, yielding syrup in spring and colorful foliage in autumn.

Jefferson to Groveton

The next segment of the drive travels 16 miles north along a series of lovely, winding back roads to **Groveton.** These can be avoided by driving on to Lancaster and heading north on US 3 to Groveton, but doing so means missing out on great adventures. To start this segment, continue 0.2 mile past the junction of US 2 and NH 116 and turn north (right) onto North Road. This rough, two-lane road runs northwest along the western edge of the Pliny Range. Rural farms with tree-lined pastures abut the tar road.

Prospect Mountain, the conical centerpiece of **John Wingate Weeks Historic Site,** rises to the west. The park, dignified by a stone tower on its summit, is named for John W. Weeks, a US senator and Cabinet member who authored and pushed through passage of the Weeks Law, which authorized the federal government to acquire and preserve forestland in the East. The law led directly to the establishment of White Mountain National Forest. Nearby 420-acre **Weeks State Park,** including the Mount Prospect estate, offers historical displays, a bird collection, information on John Weeks, and evening lectures. The mountain's summit is accessed by a fine hike, with views of the Whites and the Connecticut River Valley. The park is accessed from US 2 on the way to Lancaster.

After almost 4 miles North Road makes a sharp left turn, drops across Garland Brook, swings around Elm Ridge, and enters a residential area. After 5 miles turn right on Grange Road. The village of Grange, and all the village's residences, are reached in another 0.5 mile.

On the north side of town, the road becomes Lost Nation Road. The drive's next 10 miles follow this narrow asphalt strip along the west flank of the Pilot Range, dipping across shallow valleys, crossing gurgling brooks, and passing thick woods filled with sugar maple, beech, white birch, spruce, and fir trees or, alternately, hayfields and pastures. Cape Horn, a rounded hump, separates the highway from the unseen Connecticut River. The road finally reaches Ames Brook, bends sharply west, and descends residential streets into the mill town of Groveton. This section of the drive ends at its junction with NH 110 on the southern side of town. Turn right here to continue the drive or left to dally "downstreet" in Groveton.

Groveton lies on the north bank of the placid Upper Ammonoosuc River. Like so many northern New England communities, the town saw more prosperous days during its logging boom. Today it's a slightly depressed town of brick buildings and houses built close to its streets. The town has an industrial feel, dominated as it is by an immense paper mill and large stacks of wood chips and sawdust. On the south side of town is a 136-foot covered bridge that was built in 1852 across the river and is now restricted to foot traffic.

Groveton to the Androscoggin River

The drive's third leg runs 17 miles from Groveton to NH 16. It begins on the south bank of the river at the junction of Lost Nation Road and NH 110. Head east on NH 110. The road

A pioneer cemetery ages quietly near Stark, an old village named for Revolutionary War hero General John Stark.

follows the Upper Ammonoosuc River for a couple of miles before turning away from it and crossing a low saddle. Beach Hill, to the north, separates the highway from the river's wide bend. High forested peaks in White Mountain National Forest loom to the south, including Hutchins Mountain, North Peak, and Square Mountain.

North of the river lies a trio of state forests—Devil's Slide, Percy, and the 39,619-acre **Nash Stream Forest.** From 1900 until 1988 this area was the domain of loggers and timber companies. In the latter year it was sold to a developer. Preservationists, alarmed at the prospects, were able to acquire most of the land in the Nash Stream watershed for recreation and wildlife habitat. The area is reached via Emerson Road, 2 miles east of Groveton. Drive a logging road a dozen miles into the remote valley. Good adventures here include hiking up Percy Peaks via a 2-mile trail, trout fishing in Nash Stream, and a walk up to beautiful **Pond Brook Falls.** Here the creek tumbles in a long series of cascades and falls over polished granite benches. The falls are reached by parking at a culvert where Pond Creek crosses the road and hiking east along a trail a short distance to the lower cascades.

Back on NH 110, the drive rejoins the river valley and enters the picturesque village of **Stark.** Stark, with a white church and a 134-foot covered bridge, lies below **Devil's Slide,** a towering 800-foot cliff. The hamlet was incorporated in 1795 as Percy but later renamed for General John Stark, the Revolutionary War hero of the Battles of Bennington and Bunker Hill. Stark is also renowned for saying the famed words seen on every New Hampshire license plate—"Live Free or Die."

The village plodded along until the railroad came through in 1852 and opened up the area's vast timber reserves. The town later achieved notoriety as a World War II prisoner of war camp from 1944 to 1946. The camp's 250 inmates, captured in North Africa and Normandy, cut pulpwood for the paper industry before going home at war's end. The site of the camp, designated by a historic marker, sits just east of town along the highway. Stark hosts a lively fiddlers' contest the last Sunday of every June, concurrent with the annual "Blessing of the Bikes" farther north in Colebrook. Motorcyclists and fiddlers make this town hop that weekend.

The drive continues east up a bucolic valley that holds the meandering river, grassy pastures, and woods. An interesting pioneer cemetery sits alongside the road almost 3 miles past Stark. The highway gently ascends the valley to West Milan and its junction with NH 110A. Turn east (left) on NH 110A. The next 4 miles roll through thick spruce and fir forest, past Cedar Pond, and drop down to NH 16 and the Androscoggin River. Turn north (left) on NH 16.

The next 18-mile section of drive goes north through the Thirteen Mile Woods on a road with gorgeous backwoods scenery to Errol. The tone for the drive is set almost immediately by a road sign reading MOOSE CROSSING NEXT 17 MILES. The highway follows the west bank of the meandering **Androscoggin River,** which begins just northeast of here in Umbagog Lake on the Maine border. Androscoggin is an Indian word that means "fish curing place." Low rounded hillocks, densely wooded with spruce, fir, yellow birch, alder, and red maple, and low marshy areas flank the river and highway. The river, its flow interrupted only by Pontook Reservoir and a hydroelectric station, twists slowly between its wooded banks above the lake and plunges foamily over bedrock in short rapids below the dam.

The river offers great trout fishing, as well as canoeing and rafting on Class II and III whitewater. There are plenty of pullouts, including the **Androscoggin Wayside Park,** places to stop and picnic or watch the wildlife. Loons are often spotted on the glassy water. Listen for their unmistakable call at dusk. Moose, those ungainly symbols of the north woods, hang out in "moose stomps," obviously trampled earth, alongside the highway. Evening and early morning are the best times to spot them. Watch for them on the highway; a moose–car crash is not a pretty sight and there are no winners.

Through Dixville Notch

Errol, one of New Hampshire's northernmost villages, sits at a crossroads; two of the town's three highways head east into Maine. Errol is one of those old lumber towns that thrived during the spring timber drives when logs were driven downstream during high-water runoff. Now it relies on pulpwood cutting and serves as a supply center for outdoor recreationists exploring the backcountry. In Errol, turn west (left) onto NH 26 for the last 21 miles of the drive.

The highway quickly leaves Errol and runs northwest alongside Clear Stream up a glacier-carved valley. Akers Pond is a good-size lake adjoining the highway a mile out of town. On the south side of the road is the single strip of what is called (tongue-in-cheek) Errol International Airport—its only international flights going to nearby Canada. The valley, lorded over by darkly forested mountains, gradually constricts. The flat valley floor filled with dense thickets is prime moose territory.

At 9.7 miles from Errol, the highway enters **Dixville Notch State Park.** This 127-acre state park, traversed in only 1.5 highway miles, protects Dixville Notch, an abrupt defile sliced through ancient shales metamorphosed into schist and phyllite. Just after entering the park, look for a picnic area on the west side of the highway. After picnicking here, walk up a short trail to Huntington Cascades, a pretty series of cascades in a damp, mossy ravine. A pioneer cemetery sits by the parking lot.

Farther up the highway is another picnic area at The Flume. A short trail leads from the parking area to The Flume, a sharp granite chasm 250 feet long and 40 feet deep excavated by the rushing waters of Flume Brook. The trail winds along the gorge rim. Below the edge the brook rumbles over a series of cascades before making a 15-foot plunge off a rock ledge. Look for a 7-foot-deep pothole carved into the bedrock by swirling water.

In the state park the highway steeply climbs up a 10 percent grade through the narrowing vale into an upper canyon lined with broken cliffs and pinnacles. Finally, 11 miles from Errol, the road reaches the crest of 1,990-foot **Dixville Notch,** New Hampshire's northernmost notch and certainly its most rugged. The precipitous walls of the notch, named for early land-grant holder Timothy Dix, form an abrupt V with only enough room on its floor for the highway and a brook. The state's other notches exhibit glacial characteristics with their U-shaped contours, but Dixville Notch was sculpted by running water. One of New Hampshire's last places to be free from glacial ice, the notch is only 15,000 years old. It offers a cold, windy climate for the few hardy plants and trees clinging to its steep slopes. The trees, including white birch, red spruce, and balsam fir, are stunted by both weather and poor soil.

Park on the far west side of the notch at a southside parking area for the trailhead to **Table Rock,** a jutting rocky prow towering above the western end of the notch. The 0.3-mile trail climbs very steeply up a ravine to the crag's narrow summit platform. Table Rock yields a marvelous but hard-earned view of Dixville Notch, the surrounding mountains, and the famed resort hotel called The Balsams.

From the notch the highway drops 0.1 mile to Lake Gloriette and **The Balsams.** The latter, a grand 204-room hotel built against the stunning mountain backdrop, offers golf courses, tennis courts, a full slate of family activities, boating, swimming, and award-winning cuisine, including a heaped 100-foot buffet table in summer. *Golf Magazine* calls it "one of America's best golf resorts," while the National Trust for Historic Preservation designates it a "Historic Hotel of America." Nearby is the tiny hamlet of **Dixville Notch,** traditionally the first town to report its results in New Hampshire's presidential primary elections.

From here to Colebrook and the drive's end, NH 26 follows the gentle valley of the Mohawk River. Only 4 miles from the hotel at Kidderville is Diamond Pond Road. The road leads north 6 miles to 1,530-acre **Coleman State Park** with a 24-site campground on the spruce-forested shores of Little Diamond Pond. The lake allows fine fishing for trout.

Colebrook's Main Street is a bustling crossroads and the gateway to northern New Hampshire.

As the highway descends west, the land opens up to low, undulating hills creased by shallow valleys. Hill farms with hay-fields and dark woods are scattered alongside the highway. The road enters **Colebrook,** an old lumber town lying on the Connecticut River not far from its headwaters at the Connecticut Lakes.

Colebrook was first settled by Eleazer Rosebrook in 1774 on a land grant given to Sir George Colebrooke of the British East India Company. The town later grew and prospered with dairy-ing and potato farming. The first road through Dixville Notch in 1804 further opened the region to settlement. The Colebrook area also was the center of the logging industry during the late 19th century. Huge log drives on the Connecticut River every spring floated millions of board feet of lumber down the snowmelt-swollen river to sawmills, with as much as 100 miles of the river solidly packed with logs going to market. The log drives are now

Table Rock, reached by a short trail, offers a spectacular overview of Dixville Notch and the scenic route.

a thing of the past, and the upper Connecticut River basin has reverted back to quiet farming days with its rustic, weathered barns, dairy farms dotted with black-and-white cows, and the ever-present mountains brushed green with thick forests.

The drive quietly ends at the intersection of NH 26 and US 3 in town. Québec lies a scant 10 miles north of here. A good scenic return drive back to Groveton and Lancaster follows US 3 south along the Connecticut River through hilly countryside.

APPENDIX:
SOURCES OF MORE
INFORMATION

For more information on lands and events, please contact the following agencies and organizations.

Claremont Visitors Center
14 North St.
Claremont, NH 03743
(603) 543-1296
claremontnh.com/visitors

Franconia Notch Chamber of Commerce
PO Box 780
421 Main St.
Franconia, NH 03580
(603) 823-5661
franconianotch.org

Franconia Notch State Park
NH Route 93
Franconia, NH 03580
(603) 745-8391
nhstateparks.org

Greater Ossipee Area Chamber of Commerce
PO Box 323
Center Ossipee, NH 03814
(603) 539-6201
ossipeevalley.org

Hanover Area Chamber of Commerce
Nugget Arcade Building #216
53 South Main St.
Hanover, NH 03755
(603) 643-3115
hanoverchamber.org

Lebanon Area Chamber of Commerce
PO Box 97
1 School St., Village House
Lebanon, NH 03766
(603) 448-1203
lebanonchamber.com

Lincoln-Woodstock Chamber of Commerce
NH Route 12
Kancamagus Highway
Lincoln, NH 03251
(603) 745-6621
lincolnwoodstock.com

Littleton Area Chamber of Commerce
2 Union St.
PO Box 105
Littleton, NH 03561
(603) 444-6561
littletonareachamber.com

Mount Washington Valley Chamber of Commerce
2617 White Mountain Hwy.
North Conway, NH 03860
mtwashingtonvalley.org

New Hampshire Division of Travel and Tourism Development
PO Box 1856
172 Pembroke Rd.
Concord, NH 03302
(603) 271-2665, (800) FUN-IN-NH
visitnh.gov

Squam Lakes Area Chamber of Commerce
PO Box 665
Ashland, NH 03217
(603) 968-4494
squamlakeschamber.com

White Mountain Gateway Visitor & Interpretive Center
200 Kancamagus Hwy.
North Woodstock, NH 03262
(603) 745-3816, (800) 346-3687

White Mountain National Forest
71 White Mountain Dr.
Campton, NH 03223
(603) 536-6100

Wolfeboro Chamber of Commerce
32 Central Ave.
Wolfeboro, NH 03894
(603) 569-2200, (800) 516-5324
wolfeborochamber.com

ABOUT THE AUTHOR

Stewart M. Green, living in Colorado Springs, Colorado, is a free-lance writer and photographer for FalconGuides/Globe Pequot. He's written over 30 travel and climbing books for Globe Pequot and other publications, including *Scenic Driving Colorado, Scenic Driving Massachusetts, Scenic Driving California, KNACK Rock Climbing, Rock Climbing Colorado, Rock Climbing Europe, Rock Climbing Utah, Best Hikes Near Colorado Springs, Rock Climbing New England, Best Climbs Moab, Best Climbs Denver and Boulder,* and *Best Climbs Rocky Mountain National Park.* He's also a professional climbing guide with Front Range Climbing Company in Colorado and is the Climbing Expert at About.com. Visit him at green1109.wix.com/stewartmgreenphoto for more about his writing and photography.